STEPHEN BIESTY'S
CROSS-SECTIONS
MAN-OF-WAR

Scholastic Canada Ltd

A DORLING KINDERSLEY BOOK

Art Editor Richard Czapnik
Project Editor John C. Miles
Production Jayne Wood
Managing Editor Susan Peach
Historical Consultant Peter Goodwin
Keeper of HMS Victory

Art Director Roger Priddy

Published in Canada in 1993 by
Scholastic Canada Ltd., 123 Newkirk Road,
Richmond Hill, Ontario, Canada L4C 3G5.

Canadian Cataloguing in Publication Data

Biesty, Stephen
Cross-sections: man-of-war

ISBN 0-590-74610-3

1. Battleships - History - 18th century - Pictorial
works - Juvenile literature. 2. Battleships -
History - 18th century - Juvenile literature.
I. Platt, Richard. II. Title.

V750.B53 1993   j359.3'22   C92-095785-4

Reproduced by Dot Gradations, Essex
Printed and bound in Italy by A. Mondadori Editore, Verona

The cross-sections in this book are based on HMS *Victory*, which
was built in 1765 and fought in the Battle of Trafalgar in 1805.
She is moored at Portsmouth, England where you can visit her.

STOWAWAY

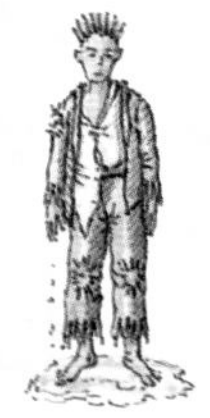

To All members of the CREW of
HIS MAJESTY'S SHIP
By Order of
THE CAPTAIN
a *generous* REWARD
of a
DOUBLED GROG RATION
will be given to
ANY MEMBER of the crew who
reports the whereabouts of a
STOWAWAY
*Seen boarding the King's Vessel the night of Wednesday
last, The cunning Rogue gaining access by the Device of
CREEPING up the Anchor Cable like a common rat.
The SCALLYWAG being no more than SEVEN years
of age, with red hair and a sulky countenance.
BEWARE the urchin bites when collared and
has a fine set of HIS OWN teeth.*

GOD SAVE THE KING

STEPHEN BIESTY'S
CROSS-SECTIONS
MAN-OF-WAR

ILLUSTRATED BY
STEPHEN BIESTY

WRITTEN BY
RICHARD PLATT

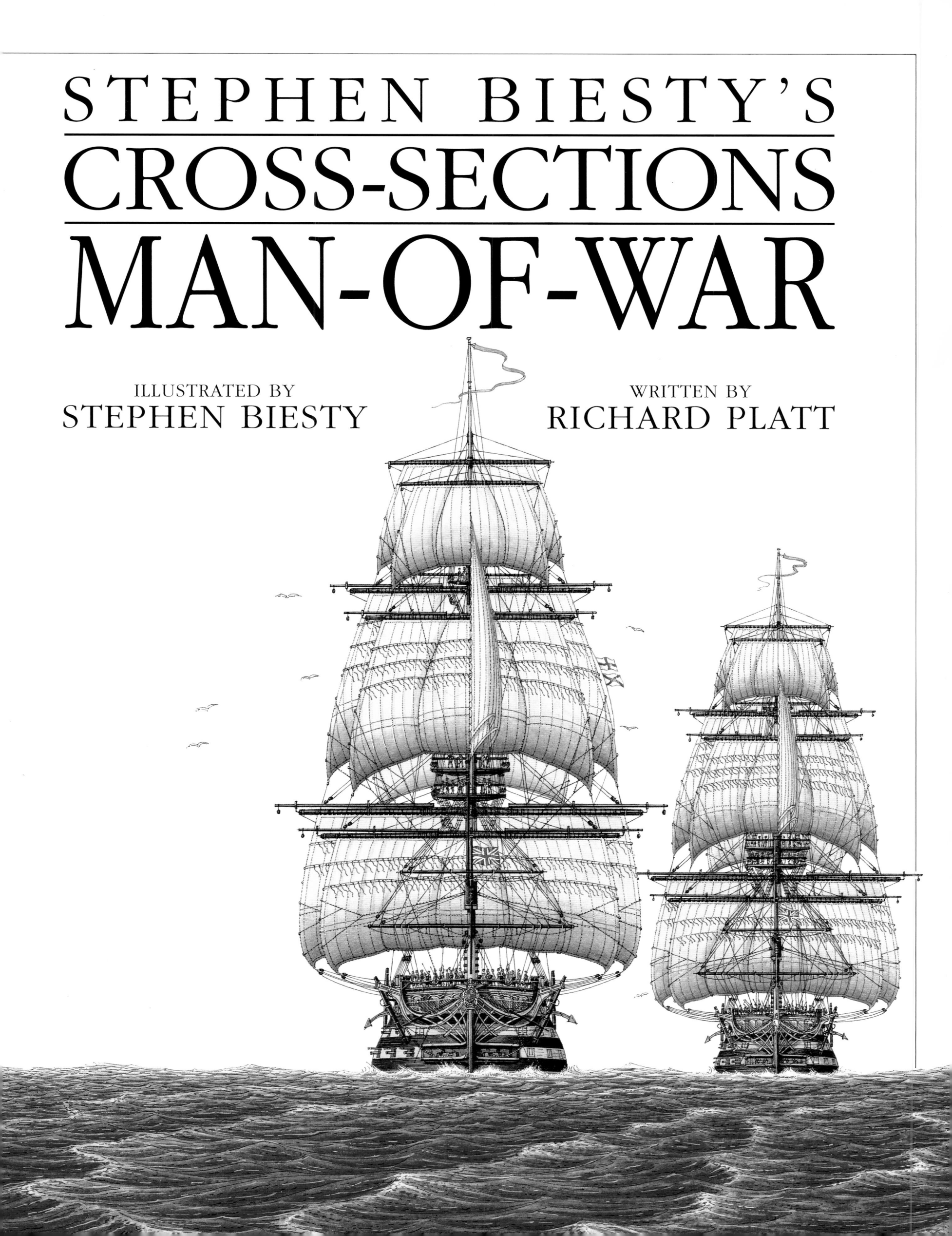

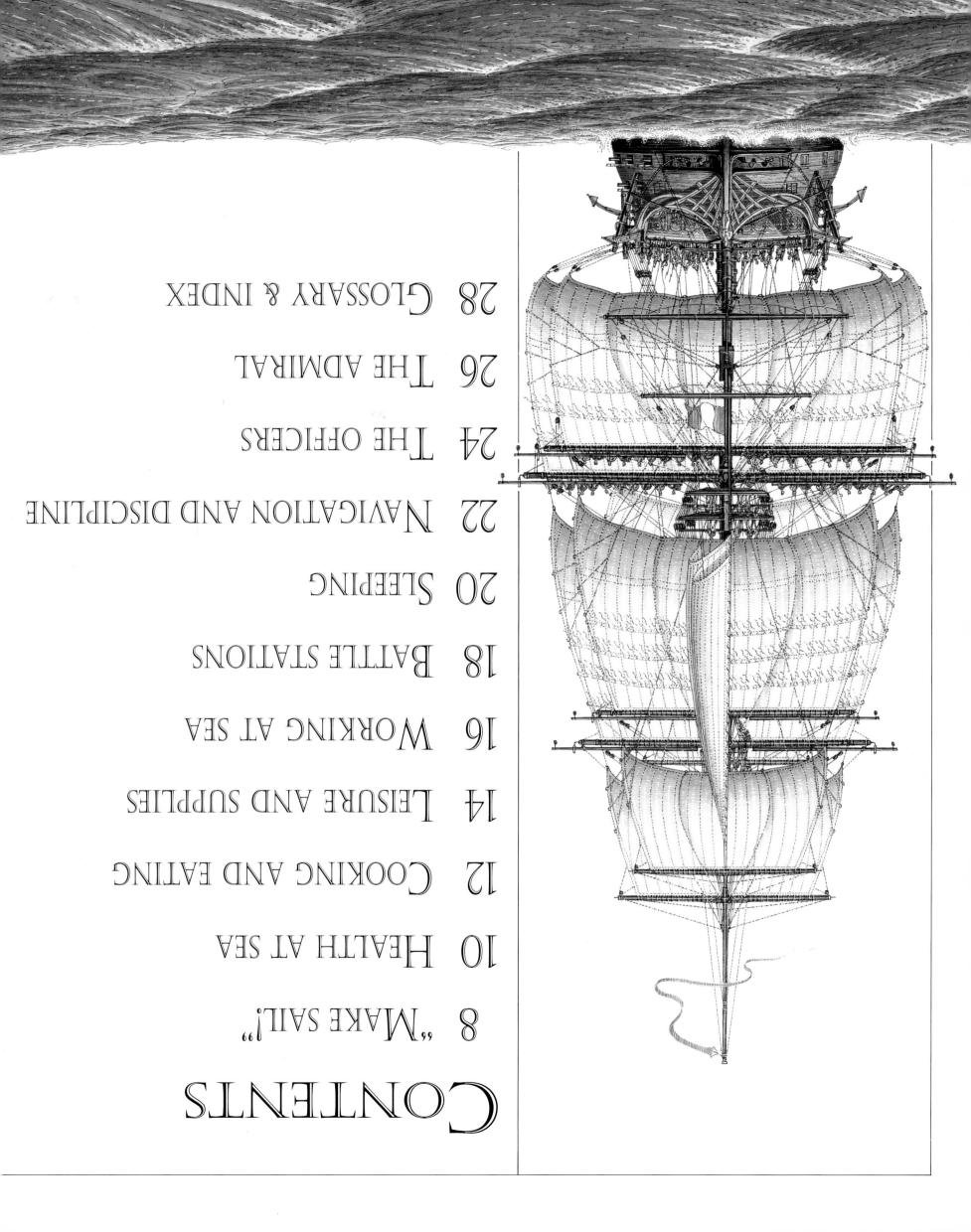

CONTENTS

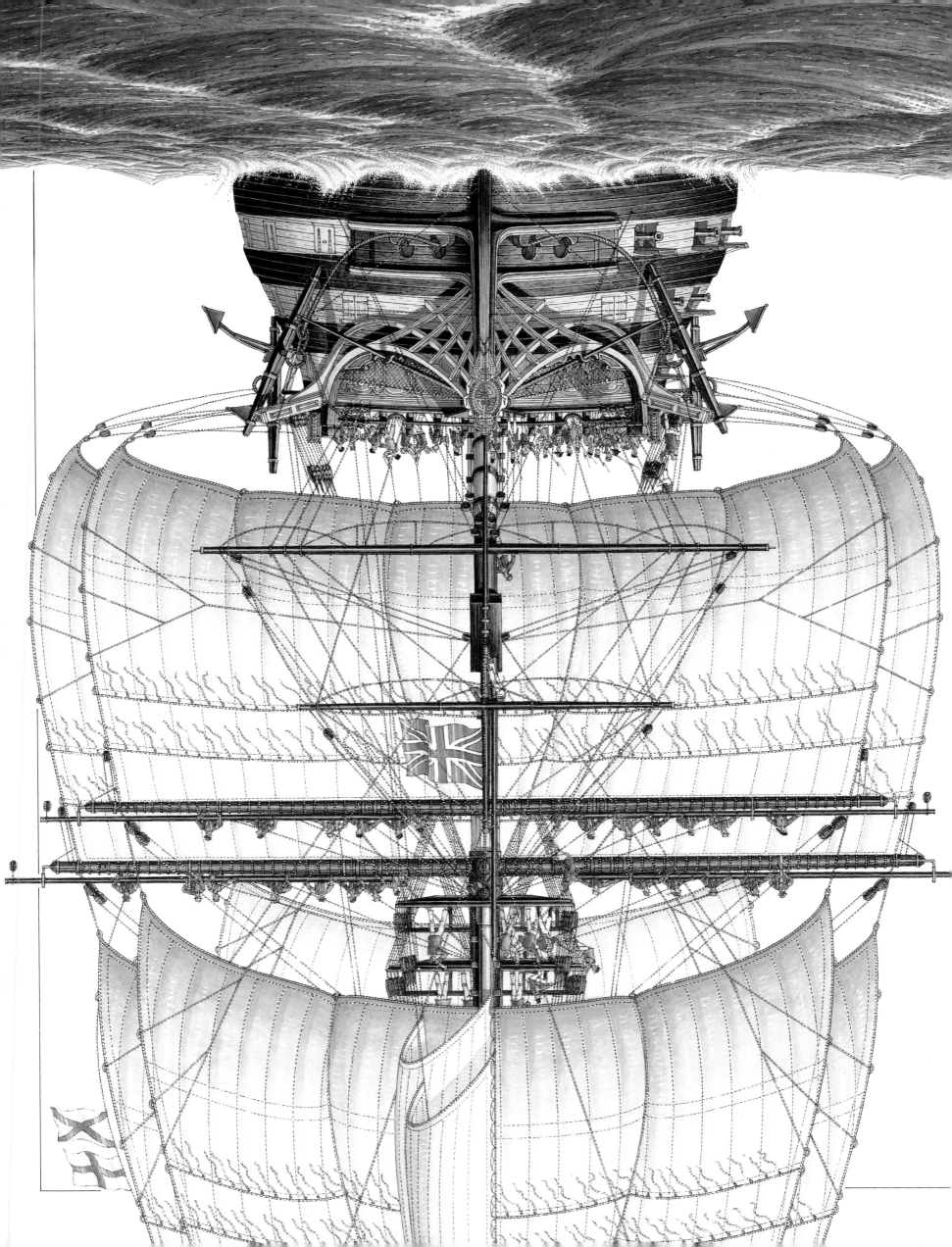

"MAKE SAIL!"

WITH THE ABOVE COMMAND, the captain of a wooden sailing warship, or "man-of-war," started a bustle of activity. Within seconds, hundreds of sailors climbed high above the rolling deck. Within minutes they unfurled huge sails to harness the power of the wind. On board, the ship carried everything the crew of about 800 needed for a voyage around the world, with a deadly battle at the end. Sea battles decided which navy – a nation's warriors at sea – controlled the oceans. The seas were the main trade routes, so the country with the strongest navy ruled the world.

Life for the ordinary sailor on board a man-of-war was very hard. He faced death from battle, accidents, and disease, and his floating home was damp, dark, and crowded. This book will take you on a section-by-section tour through a man-of-war of Great Britain's Royal Navy in about the year 1800.

This picture appears on each left-hand page. The white section tells you which part of the ship you are looking at.

THE ANATOMY OF A MAN-OF-WAR

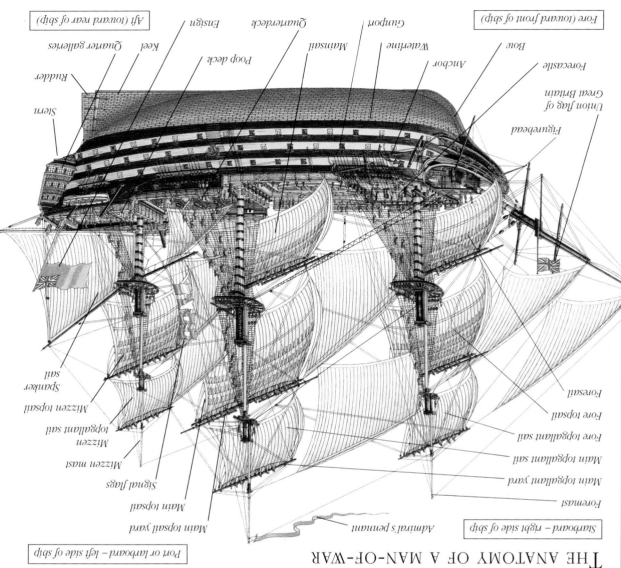

Starboard – right side of ship

Admiral's pennant

Port or larboard – left side of ship

Main topsail yard
Main topsail
Foremast
Mizzen topsail
Signal flags
Mizzen mast
Main topgallant yard
Main topgallant sail
Fore topgallant sail
Mizzen topgallant sail
Spanker sail
Fore topsail
Foresail

Stern
Rudder
Quarter galleries
Keel

Ensign
Quarterdeck
Poop deck
Mainsail
Gunport
Waterline
Anchor
Bow
Union flag of Great Britain
Figurehead
Forecastle

Aft (toward rear of ship)

Fore (toward front of ship)

A NOTE ON MEASUREMENTS

Measurements used in the Royal Navy belonged to the imperial system. Gun weights (for example, 32-pounder) and food ration units (for example, 1 lb of beef) were all measured this way. You can find metric equivalents in the text. In the non-metric system, ounce is abbreviated as oz and pound as lb. In the metric system, centimeter is abbreviated as cm and meter as m.

The picture above shows the main parts of an 18th-century wooden man-of-war. Towering above the main body of the ship, the hull, rose three huge masts – fore, main, and mizzen. These supported the yards, large horizontal poles from which the sails hung. Hundreds of ropes controlled the sails and supported the masts, making the sailing warship an incredibly complex piece of machinery.

Poop deck
The highest deck on the ship, the unarmed poop deck was used mainly by officers. From here, the signal lieutenant hauled up flag signals to nearby vessels.

Quarterdeck
At the stern of the ship, the quarterdeck was also normally reserved for the officers. From here, the captain had a good view. He slept in a cabin at the stern of the quarterdeck. Like the lower decks, the quarterdeck was armed; there were six 12-pounder cannons a side, each firing an orange-sized ball weighing 12-lb (5.5 kg).

Forecastle
This raised deck covered the main deck at the bows. Gangways linked it to the quarter deck. Many of the ship's sails were controlled from here, and there were four guns as well. Two were carronades, or "smashers," a kind of short gun firing a heavy shot. This man-of-war carried two huge 68-pounder (31-kg) carronades.

Upper gun deck
Unlike the lower and middle decks, this deck was open to the weather in the middle. Three of the man-of-war's small boats sat on cradles attached to the beams which crossed over the open space. It was armed with 24-pounder guns – 15 along each side. The admiral had his day cabin at the stern.

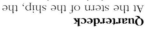

Trash
Most trash generated by the crew was simply thrown overboard.

Middle deck
The lighter 24-pounder guns on the middle deck fired smaller 24-lb (11-kg) balls, each the size of a large grapefruit. As on the lower deck, there were 14 guns on each side.

Lower deck
This was the lowest gun deck. Down each side there were fifteen 32-pounder cannons, which fired 32-lb (14-kg) balls the size of coconuts. When the ship was not fighting in a battle, many of the seamen hung their hammocks between the beams of this deck. Many of the crew slept here. The galley, the ship's kitchen, was here, too. At the stern the officers had their cabins and wardroom (dining/living room).

Orlop deck
The orlop deck got its name from a Dutch word meaning "overlap," because the deck overlapped the hold. This deck was used for storage and for the offices of some of the ship's crew who needed access to the hold, such as the purser and carpenter.

Hold
Located at the very bottom of the ship, the hold was like a giant warehouse. Here the crew stored all the provisions for the voyage – all the food and drink they needed, iron cannonballs, spare ropes and sails, and materials for repairing damage.

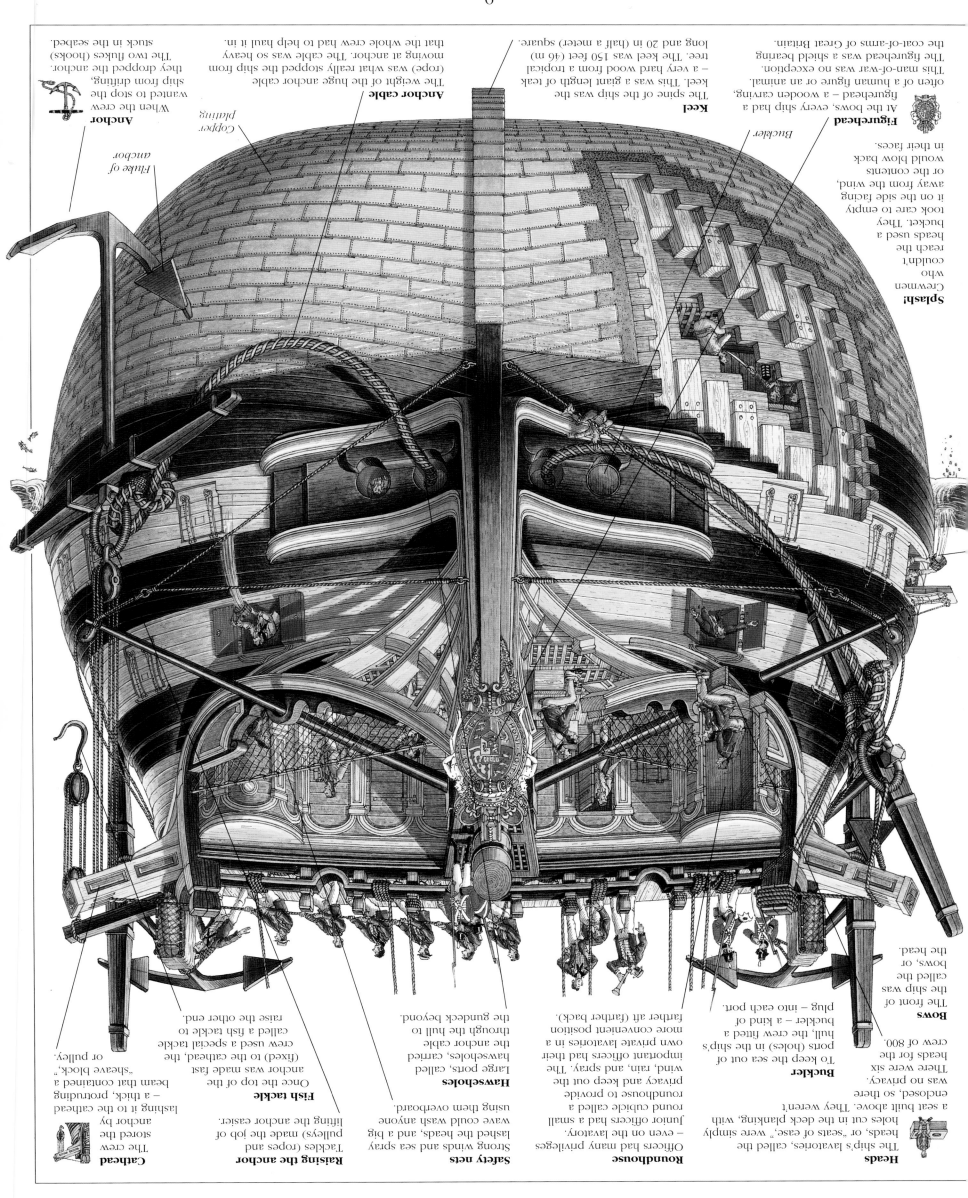

Anchor
When the crew wanted to stop the ship from drifting, they dropped the anchor. The two flukes (hooks) stuck in the seabed.

Fluke of anchor

Copper plating

Anchor cable
The weight of the huge anchor cable (rope) was what really stopped the ship from moving at anchor. The cable was so heavy that the whole crew had to help haul it in.

Keel
The spine of the ship was the keel. This was a giant length of teak – a very hard wood from a tropical tree. The keel was 150 feet (46 m) long and 20 in (half a meter) square.

Figurehead
At the bows, every ship had a figurehead – a wooden carving, often of a human figure or an animal. This man-of-war was no exception. The figurehead was a shield bearing the coat-of-arms of Great Britain.

Bucker

Splash!
Crewmen who couldn't reach the heads used a bucket. They took care to empty it on the side facing away from the wind, or the contents would blow back in their faces.

Cathead
The crew stored the anchor by lashing it to the cathead – a thick, protruding beam that contained a "sheave block," or pulley.

Fish tackle
Once the top of the anchor was made fast (fixed) to the cathead, the crew used a special tackle called a fish tackle to raise the other end.

Raising the anchor
Tackles (ropes and pulleys) made the job of lifting the anchor easier.

Safety nets
Strong winds and sea spray lashed the heads, and a big wave could wash anyone using them overboard.

Hawseholes
Large ports, called hawseholes, carried the anchor cable through the hull to the gundeck beyond.

Roundhouse
Officers had many privileges – even on the lavatory. Junior officers had a small round cubicle called a roundhouse to provide privacy and keep out the wind, rain, and spray. The important officers had their own private lavatories in a more convenient position farther aft (farther back).

Bucker
To keep the sea out of the ports (holes) in the ship's hull, the crew fitted a bucker – a kind of plug – into each port.

Bows
The front of the ship was called the bows, or the head.

Heads
The ship's lavatories, called the heads, or "seats of ease," were simply holes cut in the deck planking, with a seat built above. They weren't enclosed, so there was no privacy.

There were six heads for the crew of 800.

HEALTH AT SEA

LIFE ON BOARD A MAN-OF-WAR was riddled with health hazards. Sailors accepted some risks, such as enemy fire or falls from the rigging, as part of the job. But what they feared most was disease. Disease killed slowly and was more deadly. For each seaman killed in action, as many as 40 died of disease. Medical science was primitive. Even doctors did not fully understand why fevers spread so rapidly. They knew that crowding was part of the problem. Dirt and damp didn't help. It was almost impossible for the men to wash themselves or their clothes properly. Soap was not issued to seamen until about 1825. To get their clothes clean, the crew soaked them in urine, then rinsed them in seawater! Despite these health risks, sailors were probably sick no more often than their friends on land, who could not afford the regular meals or medical attention that sailors enjoyed.

SCURVY

Pale skin

Sunken eyes

Loss of teeth

The symptoms of the disease called scurvy included gradual weakening, pale skin, sunken eyes, tender gums, muscle pain, loss of teeth, internal bleeding, and the opening of wounds such as sword cuts that had healed many years before. Exhaustion, fainting, diarrhea, and lung and kidney trouble followed. Eventually, the sailor "went to Davy Jones's locker" (naval slang for dying).

Lemons and limes

Turnips

Cabbage

Carrots

Onions

Scurvy was much rarer in 1800 than it had been 50 years previously, and the disease affected the crew only on long journeys. Although doctors hadn't yet discovered the cause of scurvy (lack of vitamin C), naval commanders found that fresh fruit and vegetables kept scurvy from their crews. Fruit and vegetables contain vitamin C, so scurvy was beaten by giving the crew fresh vegetables when available, sauerkraut (pickled cabbage), or lemons and limes.

THE SURGEON AND HIS TOOLS

Ships' surgeons varied widely in ability. They were important in battles, when they had to amputate (cut off) smashed arms and legs. Speed was vital, because quick work reduced the risk of infection, which killed more men than the surgery itself.

RUM
The surgeon's patients were given rum to numb the pain, because amputations were done without anesthetics.

KNIVES
Razor sharp knives cut through skin, muscles, and ligaments to reach bones.

GAG
Victims were given a gag made of rope or leather to bite on as another way of dulling the agonizing pain. Mercifully, the victim usually fainted.

BONE SAW
Fine, sharp saws cut through leg and arm bones. These were standard tools in the surgeon's kit.

BOILING PITCH
After the amputation, the bloody arm or leg stump was dipped in boiling pitch (tar) to seal the wound and stop the bleeding.

PEG LEG
The amputee was given a wooden leg so he could walk again.

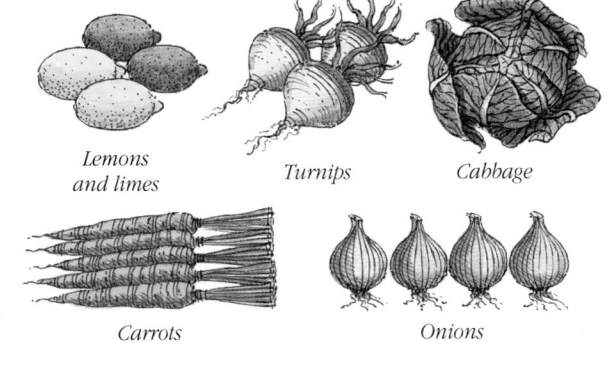

Washing hammocks
Washing hammocks was essential for health, but took up lots of room. The crew took turns scrubbing their hammocks whenever the weather was good enough to dry them.

The sick bay
Medical treatment for the sick was primitive. On many ships, the only advantage of the sick bay was that it separated the sick men from their healthy companions.

Cat head
These beams were called cat heads because the ends were originally carved into the shape of a cat's, or lion's, head.

Bible bashing
To scrub the decks, sailors used blocks of stone. They were the size and shape of big family bibles, so they were nicknamed "holystones."

Pool
In tropical waters, the crew rigged a sail over the side to form a shark-proof swimming pool.

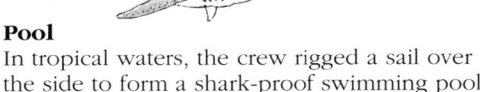

Tropical diseases
The most unhealthy places to sail to were the tropical ports. The worst year was 1726: Admiral Hosier's expedition set out with 4,750 men, and 4,000 of them died of disease.

Scrubbing the decks
The ritual of cleaning the deck took place every morning. It was more like sandpapering than washing, because the holystones slid on a mixture of sand and water that the midshipmen sprinkled. After rinsing, the upper decks dried quickly, but the constant washing kept the lower decks permanently damp.

Overcrowding
The crew lived, worked, and slept in cramped, airless conditions. The lower decks were especially badly ventilated and smelled strongly of sweaty bodies.

"Ouch! my head!"
Low beams meant sailors had to stoop constantly. Some people thought that sailors went crazy because they banged their heads so often.

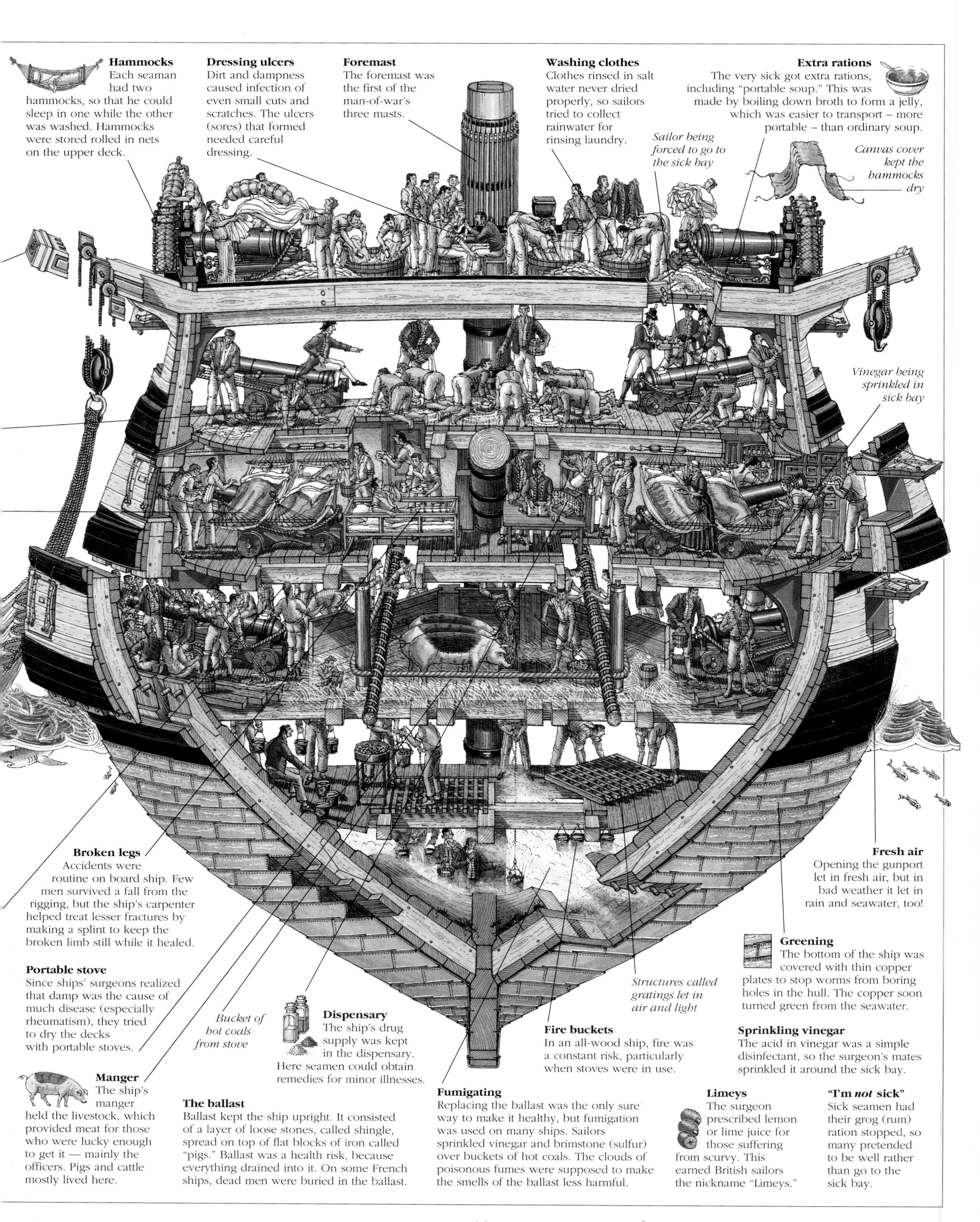

Hammocks
Each seaman had two hammocks, so that he could sleep in one while the other was washed. Hammocks were stored rolled in nets on the upper deck.

Dressing ulcers
Dirt and dampness caused infection of even small cuts and scratches. The ulcers (sores) that formed needed careful dressing.

Foremast
The foremast was the first of the man-of-war's three masts.

Washing clothes
Clothes rinsed in salt water never dried properly, so sailors tried to collect rainwater for rinsing laundry.

Extra rations
The very sick got extra rations, including "portable soup." This was made by boiling down broth to form a jelly, which was easier to transport – more portable – than ordinary soup.

Sailor being forced to go to the sick bay

Canvas cover kept the hammocks dry

Vinegar being sprinkled in sick bay

Broken legs
Accidents were routine on board ship. Few men survived a fall from the rigging, but the ship's carpenter helped treat lesser fractures by making a splint to keep the broken limb still while it healed.

Portable stove
Since ships' surgeons realized that damp was the cause of much disease (especially rheumatism), they tried to dry the decks with portable stoves.

Manger
The ship's manger held the livestock, which provided meat for those who were lucky enough to get it — mainly the officers. Pigs and cattle mostly lived here.

Bucket of hot coals from stove

Dispensary
The ship's drug supply was kept in the dispensary. Here seamen could obtain remedies for minor illnesses.

The ballast
Ballast kept the ship upright. It consisted of a layer of loose stones, called shingle, spread on top of flat blocks of iron called "pigs." Ballast was a health risk, because everything drained into it. On some French ships, dead men were buried in the ballast.

Fumigating
Replacing the ballast was the only sure way to make it healthy, but fumigation was used on many ships. Sailors sprinkled vinegar and brimstone (sulfur) over buckets of hot coals. The clouds of poisonous fumes were supposed to make the smells of the ballast less harmful.

Structures called gratings let in air and light

Fire buckets
In an all-wood ship, fire was a constant risk, particularly when stoves were in use.

Fresh air
Opening the gunport let in fresh air, but in bad weather it let in rain and seawater, too!

Greening
The bottom of the ship was covered with thin copper plates to stop worms from boring holes in the hull. The copper soon turned green from the seawater.

Sprinkling vinegar
The acid in vinegar was a simple disinfectant, so the surgeon's mates sprinkled it around the sick bay.

Limeys
The surgeon prescribed lemon or lime juice for those suffering from scurvy. This earned British sailors the nickname "Limeys."

"I'm *not* sick"
Sick seamen had their grog (rum) ration stopped, so many pretended to be well rather than go to the sick bay.

COOKING AND EATING

READ THE SHIP'S MENU, and you'd never guess that the food was one of the attractions of joining the navy. Meals included: rotting, stinking meat; biscuits riddled with maggots; and cheese so tough that sailors carved it into buttons for their uniforms. The drink was just as bad. The "fresh" water soon turned to green slime, and the beer kept little better.

Meals tasted bad because it was very hard to keep food fresh. Voyages could last years, and there was no refrigeration. The ship usually carried live animals for food, but their meat, milk, and eggs were mostly reserved for the officers. Meat for the seamen was stored in salt, which made it dry and very tough. Bread turned stale or moldy, so the navy issued hard biscuits made of flour and water instead. Despite all this, shipboard food was probably better than the food sailors ate with their families at home.

THE À LA CARTE MENU

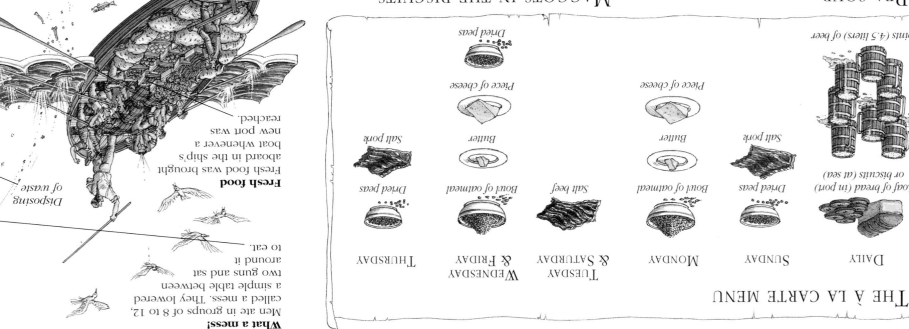

DAILY	SUNDAY	MONDAY	TUESDAY & SATURDAY	WEDNESDAY & FRIDAY	THURSDAY
Loaf of bread (in port) or biscuits (at sea)	Salt pork	Bowl of oatmeal	Salt beef	Bowl of oatmeal	Salt pork
8 pints (4.5 liters) of beer	Dried peas	Butter		Butter	Dried peas
	Piece of cheese	Piece of cheese		Dried peas	

THE COOK

Each mess marked its meat with a metal tag

The ship's cook was often one-legged, because it was one of the few jobs a disabled seaman could do and remain in the navy. He was nicknamed "slushy" after the slush – the yellow grease that floated to the top of the pan in which the fatty salt meat cooked. The cook sold slush to the crew to spread on their biscuits, because the butter which the navy supplied was often rancid (stale) when it reached the ship.

PEA SOUP

Dried peas were usually made into soup. This was the one meal that the sailors didn't complain about. The tedious routine of food varied a little when the ship was close to land. The purser then bought fresh vegetables, as this kept the scurvy away.

MAGGOTS IN THE BISCUITS

Crew members shared their biscuits with rats, maggots, and insects called weevils. They called the maggots "bargemen," joking that the biscuit was the barge, and the maggot was sailing it. Rats were easy to identify, and you'd notice one if you bit into it. The other two were less noticeable. One sailor said, "black-headed maggots were very fat and cold, but not bitter... like weevils."

Maggots in a piece of biscuit

GETTING RID OF MAGGOTS

1. Put a large dead fish onto the sack of biscuits, and the maggots crawl out to eat it.
2. When maggots cover the fish, throw fish in sea and replace with a fresh one.
3. Repeat steps 1 & 2 until no more maggots appear.

Fuel store
The galley stove burned wood and coal. To keep the fuel dry the store was at the side of the hold, above the level of the bilges.

Steward's room
The steward brought supplies of salt beef, dried peas, oatmeal, and biscuits up from the hold. His mate measured them out from open casks for the waiting mess cooks.

Messmates
Sailors messed together for the whole voyage, so messmates became close friends, almost like brothers. They took turns being mess "cook." The cook drew the rations for the mess from the ship's stores and prepared them for cooking. At mealtime one of the mess turned his back and decided who got each plate. This ensured that everyone got a fair share, because he couldn't see how big the portions were.

Greasy scarves
Sailor's neck scarves got very greasy because they wiped their hands on them.

Disposing of waste

Fresh food
Fresh food was brought aboard in the ship's boat whenever a new port was reached.

What a mess!
Men ate in groups of 8 to 12, called a mess. They lowered a simple table between two guns and sat around it to eat.

The steep tub
Meat had to soak in water before cooking, to remove the salt that preserved it. Each piece was soaked, or steeped, in the steep tub.

The purser
Supplying food, clothing, and bedding was the purser's responsibility. He kept track of how much everyone used and accounted for it at the end of the voyage. He also kept an account of the crew's pay. The purser was paid very little himself, and he had to sell food and other things at a profit. The purser was not popular, because everyone suspected him of getting rich by stealing. Often they were right!

Timekeeping
Most ships kept time using a half-hour sand-glass, like a big eggtimer. The quartermaster's mate rang the bell each time he turned the glass to measure the next half-hour.

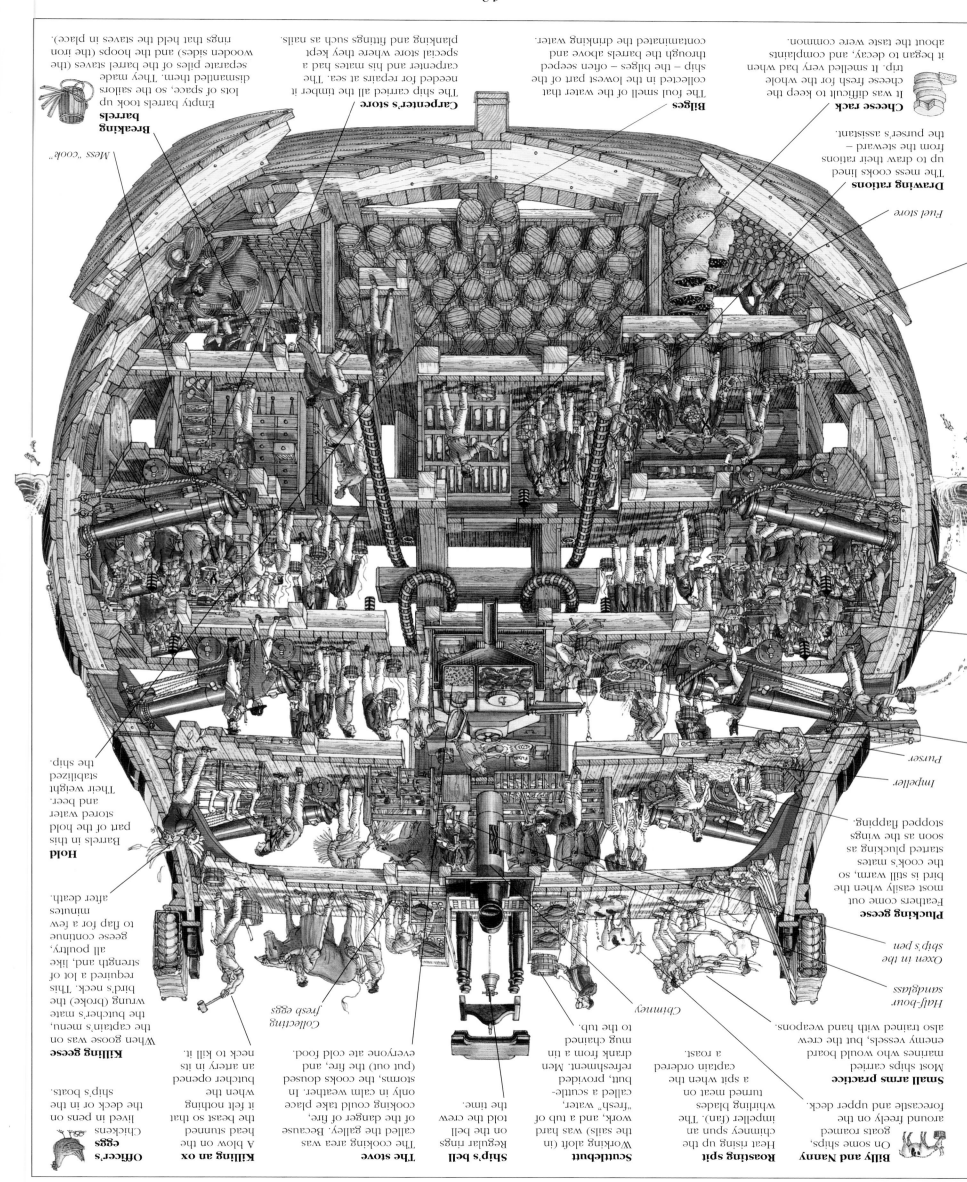

Breaking barrels
Empty barrels took up lots of space, so the sailors dismantled them. They made separate piles of the barrel staves (the wooden sides) and the iron rings that held the staves in place).

Mess "cook"

Carpenter's store
The ship carried all the timber it needed for repairs at sea. The carpenter and his mates had a special store where they kept planking and fittings such as nails.

Bilges
The foul smell of the water that collected in the lowest part of the ship – the bilges – often seeped through the barrels above and contaminated the drinking water.

Cheese rack
It was difficult to keep the cheese fresh for the whole trip. It smelled very bad when it began to decay, and complaints about the taste were common.

Drawing rations
The mess cooks lined up to draw their rations from the steward – the purser's assistant.

Fuel store

Hold
Barrels in this part of the hold stored water and beer. Their weight stabilized the ship.

Purser

Impeller

Plucking geese
Feathers come out most easily when the bird is still warm, so the cook's mates started plucking as soon as the wings stopped flapping.

Oxen in the ship's pen

Half-hour sandglass

Small arms practice
Most ships carried marines who would board enemy vessels, but the crew also trained with hand weapons.

Killing geese
When goose was on the captain's menu, the butcher's mate wrung (broke) the bird's neck. This required a lot of strength and, like all poultry, geese continue to flap for a few minutes after death.

Officer's eggs
Chickens lived in pens on the deck or in the ship's boats.

Killing an ox
A blow on the head stunned the beast so that it felt nothing when the butcher opened an artery in its neck to kill it.

The stove
The cooking area was called the galley. Because of the danger of fire, cooking could take place only in calm weather. In storms, the cooks doused (put out) the fire, and everyone ate cold food.

Ship's bell
Regular rings on the bell told the crew the time.

Collecting fresh eggs

Scuttlebutt
Working aloft (in the sails) was hard work, and a tub of "fresh" water, called a scuttle-butt, provided refreshment. Men drank from a tin mug chained to the tub.

Chimney

Roasting spit
Heat rising up the chimney spun an impeller (fan). The whirling blades turned meat on a spit when the captain ordered a roast.

Billy and Nanny
On some ships, goats roamed around freely on the forecastle and upper deck.

LEISURE AND SUPPLIES

EVERY SAILOR LOOKED FORWARD to a spell in port. It meant that the ship could take on fresh supplies. Fresh meat, bread, fruit, and vegetables made a change from the usual boring rations. But more important, being in port meant the chance of leave (holiday). Sailors spent months at a time obeying orders and living close together on crowded decks. They had little leisure time at sea. They longed for the opportunity to escape navy discipline and let themselves go. In port, they dressed up in their best shore clothes and drew their pay. Then most went ashore and spent it on getting drunk – preferably in the company of beautiful women. The sailors had a good time in port, even if they didn't get shore leave. Traders came on board with local women and fresh food. While the ship was in port, the lower decks resembled a wild party, with drinking, dancing, and antics day and night.

THE PRESS GANG

Getting recruits (new sailors) for the navy in wartime was always a problem, because not enough men volunteered. So in port, the ship sent out a press gang. This was a group of 8 to 12 men who tried to persuade seamen they met on shore to join the navy. If the men didn't want to join, the press gang took them prisoner and pressed (forced) them into the navy. The press gang was very unpopular, because once on board, there was no escape for the pressed man.

THE FLEET REGATTA

When the fleet anchored in safe waters, the crews of all the men-of-war used their leisure time to stage a regatta. This was a seagoing carnival day, with races and a nautical fancy-dress parade. The crews dressed up the ship's boats as exotic craft such as Chinese junks and raced them, perhaps paddling with shovels. The sailors collected money from each ship, and the fastest team won it all.

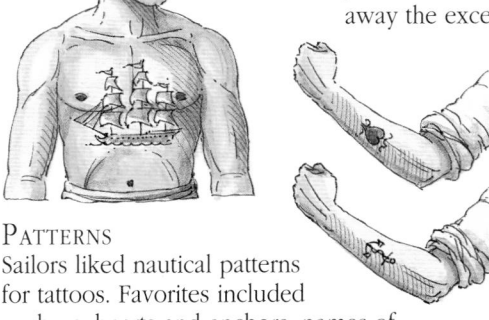

TATTOOING

Sailors first saw tattoos decorating the bodies of Pacific Island people, and they copied the custom themselves. They used needles to prick out patterns in the skin. Rubbing ink or even ash into the wound made a permanent mark. A good tatooist could use his skills to earn extra money from his shipmates.

inks
needle
ink bottle
cloth

TOOLS OF THE TRADE
Tattoo tools included needles, colored inks, and a cloth to wipe away the excess ink.

PATTERNS
Sailors liked nautical patterns for tattoos. Favorites included anchors, hearts-and-anchors, names of sweethearts, and, more elaborately, ships. Some sailors eventually had their whole bodies tattooed.

Exotic pets
In foreign ports, sailors bought unusual pets for their sweethearts, or to sell. Parrots were so popular that "bag, hammock, and birdcage" was naval slang for a sailor's possessions.

A sailor ashore
It wasn't difficult to recognize a sailor ashore. His sunburn, tattoos, and strange language set the sailor on leave apart. But the fact that he was so drunk that he couldn't stand up was the surest guide!

Parbuckling
To haul casks on board ship, the crew sometimes used a parbuckle – they looped ropes around the barrel and rolled it up the ship's side.

Floating the barrels
Barrels and casks coming aboard ship were floated to the side of the ship, where they could be hauled aboard.

Sailors waving to their sweethearts

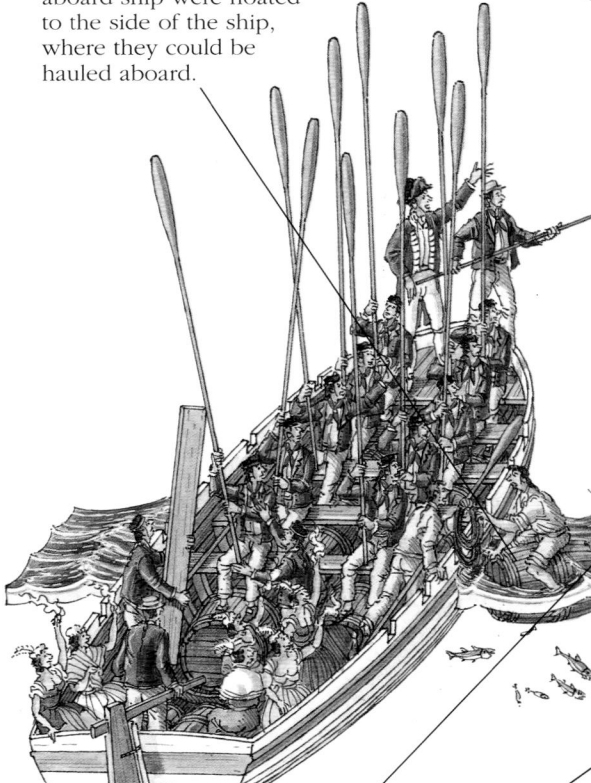

Striking a bargain
Traders who boarded the ship knew what caught a sailor's eye. They packed colorful, gaudy fabric and ribbon, shiny shoe buckles, and cheap jewelry.

Gambling
Betting was illegal, but it still went on. A favorite game was "crown and anchor," played with a round board and three special dice. Fistfights provided another opportunity for gambling. The crowd placed bets on who would win.

Paying off
The navy paid wages in full only when seamen left the navy, or transferred to another ship. Until then, sailors received part in cash, and part in "tickets" – vouchers that they could exchange for goods.

Sea chests
Some crew members kept their shore clothes in sea chests. Several messmates often shared a chest. Chests were stowed away most of the time, and the seamen had few personal possessions in daily use.

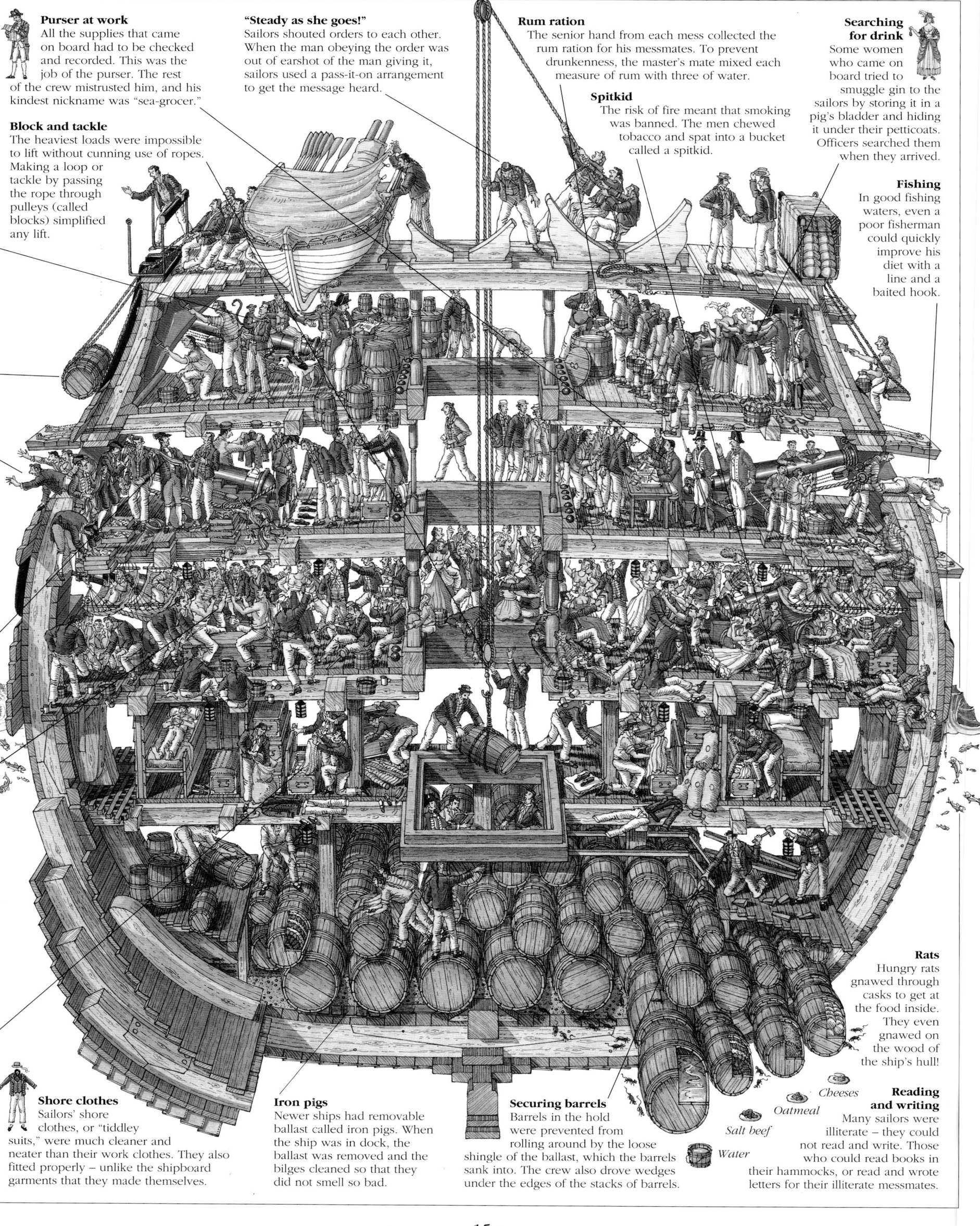

Purser at work
All the supplies that came on board had to be checked and recorded. This was the job of the purser. The rest of the crew mistrusted him, and his kindest nickname was "sea-grocer."

Block and tackle
The heaviest loads were impossible to lift without cunning use of ropes. Making a loop or tackle by passing the rope through pulleys (called blocks) simplified any lift.

"Steady as she goes!"
Sailors shouted orders to each other. When the man obeying the order was out of earshot of the man giving it, sailors used a pass-it-on arrangement to get the message heard.

Rum ration
The senior hand from each mess collected the rum ration for his messmates. To prevent drunkenness, the master's mate mixed each measure of rum with three of water.

Spitkid
The risk of fire meant that smoking was banned. The men chewed tobacco and spat into a bucket called a spitkid.

Searching for drink
Some women who came on board tried to smuggle gin to the sailors by storing it in a pig's bladder and hiding it under their petticoats. Officers searched them when they arrived.

Fishing
In good fishing waters, even a poor fisherman could quickly improve his diet with a line and a baited hook.

Rats
Hungry rats gnawed through casks to get at the food inside. They even gnawed on the wood of the ship's hull!

Shore clothes
Sailors' shore clothes, or "tiddley suits," were much cleaner and neater than their work clothes. They also fitted properly – unlike the shipboard garments that they made themselves.

Iron pigs
Newer ships had removable ballast called iron pigs. When the ship was in dock, the ballast was removed and the bilges cleaned so that they did not smell so bad.

Securing barrels
Barrels in the hold were prevented from rolling around by the loose shingle of the ballast, which the barrels sank into. The crew also drove wedges under the edges of the stacks of barrels.

Cheeses

Oatmeal

Salt beef

Water

Reading and writing
Many sailors were illiterate – they could not read and write. Those who could read books in their hammocks, or read and wrote letters for their illiterate messmates.

WORKING AT SEA

A MAN-OF-WAR AT SEA needed constant attention. The helmsman at the wheel had to make sure he steered the ship on the correct course, but there were many other jobs, too. For example, just the right combination of sails had to be rigged. Too little sail, and the ship didn't move fast enough through the water. Too much sail, and a strong gust of wind might snap a mast. To trim (adjust) a sail, the crew had to climb to the yard (the horizontal bar that supported the sail), and either make sail (increase the area of sail that caught the wind) or furl (roll up) the sail. The fastest crews could put full sail on a man-of-war in just six minutes. Other work included the daily routine of cleaning, maintenance, and preparation for battle.

Sew-sew boys
Seamen made and mended their own clothes – this was usually a Saturday ritual. Members of the crew who were especially good with a needle were called "sew-sew boys," and mended officers' clothes for them.

A fall from the rigging
Sailors worked aloft with no safety nets or other protection against falls. In the rush to loose sails, it was easy to make mistakes, with fatal results. Nobody ever suffered slight injuries from a fall: Either they plunged into the icy sea or broke their bodies on the deck below. Despite the risks, many experienced sailors ran along the top of the yards to get into position and then dropped onto the footropes below!

Lubber's hole
Most sailors clambered around the fighting top (platform) halfway up the mast. For those who felt insecure, however, there was a safer way up, close to the mast, called the "lubber's hole."

Furling sails
When a sail was not in use, the topmen tied it up below the yard. They tried to furl the sail neatly, because everyone on the ship could see the furled sail high up in the rigging. However, in a strong wind it wasn't easy to gather the wet, flapping canvas and tie it in orderly folds.

Loosing sails
To make the ship go faster, the topmen (the men who worked aloft) unrolled the sails to catch more wind. On the command "let fall," they released a sail, taking care to unfurl it first at the yard-arm (the tips of the yard), and only then at the bunt (the middle). Loosing the bunt first allowed wind to fill the sail too soon, so that it rose above the yard. The full sail could easily knock the man at the yardarm off his perch.

Going aloft
Even in harbor you had to be fit to climb the ratlines (rope ladders). But seamen also had to go aloft in gales, at night, and with ice coating every rope.

Sea chanteys
Music lightened the heavy work. The crew sang sea chanteys — work songs that had a very strong rhythm. On the beat, the men heaved. Everyone sang the chorus, and a chanteyman made up the verses as he went along. Often the chanteyman made fun of the officers in his songs by calling them rude names. The officers didn't mind as long as the chanteys helped the men heave harder on the capstan.

Capstan
All hands helped with heavy work. The most difficult task was hauling in the anchor cable. The crew used a capstan (a big winch) for this. They turned the capstan with heavy wooden capstan bars.

Caulking the decks
Cracks between deck planks could let in water, so they were stopped up by caulking. This meant hammering oakum (unraveled rope fibers) into the cracks and sealing them with pitch (tar).

Extra sails called "stunsails" were attached to these booms

Checking the gunlock
The firing mechanism of the gun (called a gunlock) was delicate and needed special attention. When the gun was not in use, the crew protected the gunlock with a lead cover.

Manhandling
The huge anchor cable was made of hemp. It was very heavy, especially when wet. To prevent the cable from rotting, the crew stored it on a special slatted floor that allowed the water to drain off the cable and air to circulate.

Footropes supported crew members working aloft

Away aloft
On the order "away aloft," the men scurried up the ratlines into the rigging. These were pieces of rope tied like rungs of a ladder between the the shrouds – the ropes that supported the mast. Climbing all the way to the topgallant (the highest yard) was exhausting. Often, the last man to reach his post would be whipped for his slowness.

Sails were made from 2-ft (60-cm)-wide lengths of linen

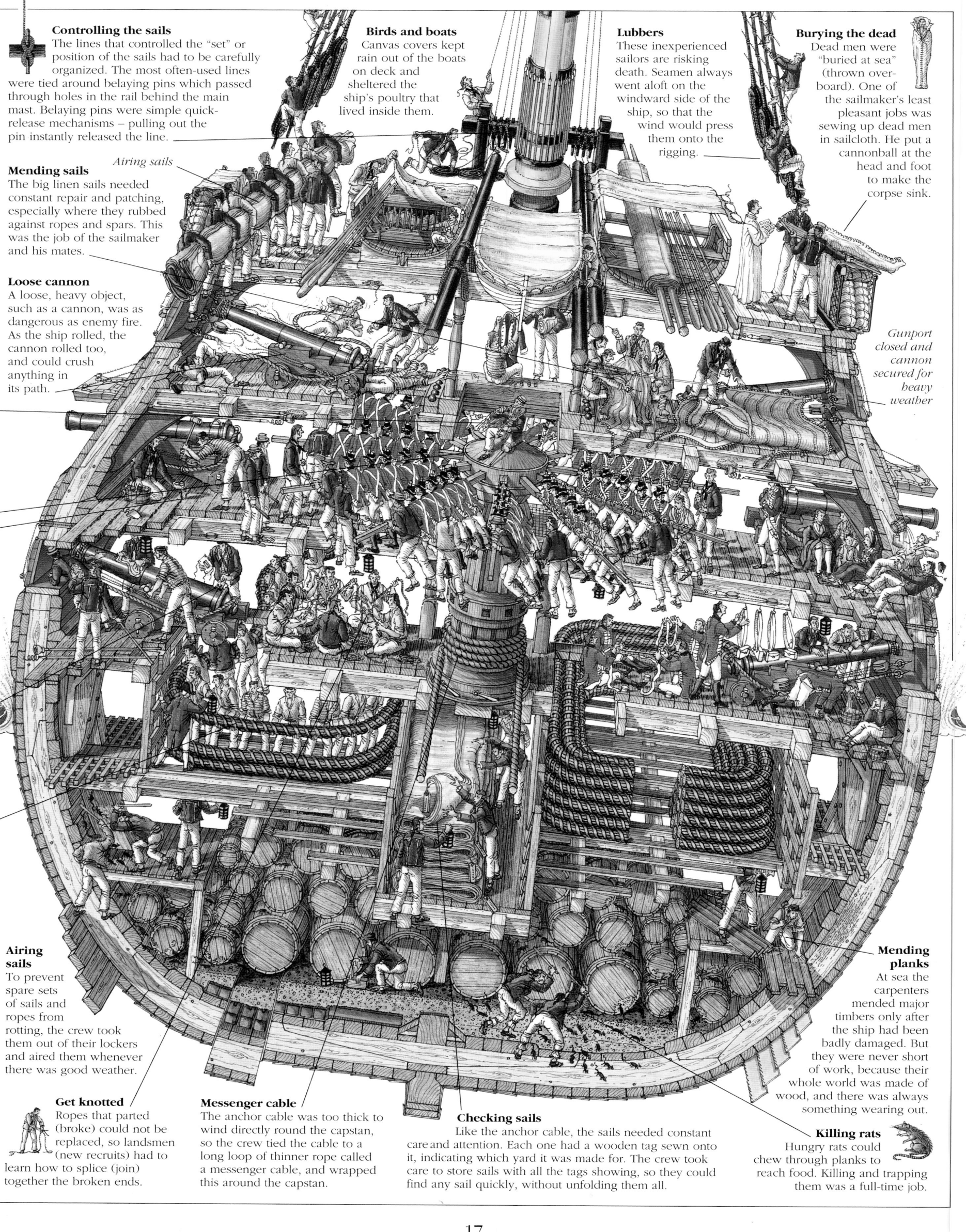

Controlling the sails
The lines that controlled the "set" or position of the sails had to be carefully organized. The most often-used lines were tied around belaying pins which passed through holes in the rail behind the main mast. Belaying pins were simple quick-release mechanisms – pulling out the pin instantly released the line.

Airing sails

Mending sails
The big linen sails needed constant repair and patching, especially where they rubbed against ropes and spars. This was the job of the sailmaker and his mates.

Loose cannon
A loose, heavy object, such as a cannon, was as dangerous as enemy fire. As the ship rolled, the cannon rolled too, and could crush anything in its path.

Birds and boats
Canvas covers kept rain out of the boats on deck and sheltered the ship's poultry that lived inside them.

Lubbers
These inexperienced sailors are risking death. Seamen always went aloft on the windward side of the ship, so that the wind would press them onto the rigging.

Burying the dead
Dead men were "buried at sea" (thrown overboard). One of the sailmaker's least pleasant jobs was sewing up dead men in sailcloth. He put a cannonball at the head and foot to make the corpse sink.

Gunport closed and cannon secured for heavy weather

Airing sails
To prevent spare sets of sails and ropes from rotting, the crew took them out of their lockers and aired them whenever there was good weather.

Mending planks
At sea the carpenters mended major timbers only after the ship had been badly damaged. But they were never short of work, because their whole world was made of wood, and there was always something wearing out.

Get knotted
Ropes that parted (broke) could not be replaced, so landsmen (new recruits) had to learn how to splice (join) together the broken ends.

Messenger cable
The anchor cable was too thick to wind directly round the capstan, so the crew tied the cable to a long loop of thinner rope called a messenger cable, and wrapped this around the capstan.

Checking sails
Like the anchor cable, the sails needed constant care and attention. Each one had a wooden tag sewn onto it, indicating which yard it was made for. The crew took care to store sails with all the tags showing, so they could find any sail quickly, without unfolding them all.

Killing rats
Hungry rats could chew through planks to reach food. Killing and trapping them was a full-time job.

17

BATTLE STATIONS

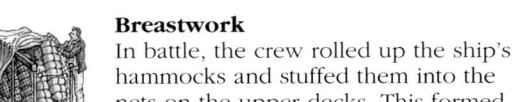

GOING INTO BATTLE on a wooden warship was both an exciting and terrifying experience. The cries of wounded comrades and the booms of cannon fire drowned out the sounds of creaking timbers and flapping canvas. The smell of blood and burning gunpowder hid the comforting smells of tar and the sea. But especially frightening was how close the enemy ships came before a single shot rang out. The ship's guns had tremendous destructive power, but they were only accurate at short range. So, tension grew as the ships sailed closer and closer, holding their fire until they were sure it would be deadly. When the ships had sailed close enough for their fire to be effective, each would try to be the first to fire a broadside – a huge blast from all the guns on one side of a ship firing together. The massive power of a broadside could often cripple the enemy at the start of a battle.

BATTLE RAGES

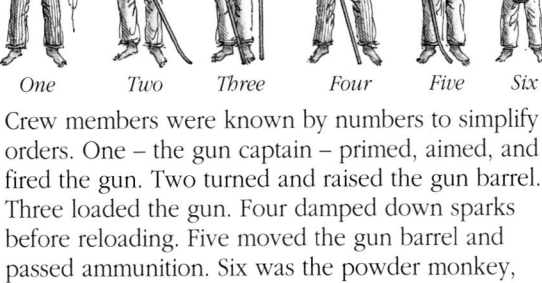

When cannon balls holed the ship's hull, carpenters worked quickly to repair the damage. Few ships sank in battle. More often, gunfire killed the crew or destroyed the rigging, thus disabling the ship. If all else failed, the crew would attack by boarding the enemy ship. Hand guns took so long to reload that, after one shot, seamen would continue fighting with pikes, knives, and hatchets.

SIX-MAN GUN CREW

| One | Two | Three | Four | Five | Six |

Crew members were known by numbers to simplify orders. One – the gun captain – primed, aimed, and fired the gun. Two turned and raised the gun barrel. Three loaded the gun. Four damped down sparks before reloading. Five moved the gun barrel and passed ammunition. Six was the powder monkey, who delivered fresh gunpowder. Powder monkeys were often the youngest members of the crew – some of them boys only 10 or 12 years old!

FIRING A CANNON

Gun crews worked very quickly. It took them only two to five minutes to clean, load, aim, and fire a cannon!

1 After firing, the crew cleaned the gun and damped down sparks to prevent an explosion during re-loading. They loaded the gun with shot and gunpowder and inserted a quill filled with powder as a fuse.

2 The crew used handspikes and ropes to lever the gun into firing position. Then they waited for the ship's roll to point the gun up, to shoot at the enemy ship's rigging, or down, to aim at its hull.

3 As the gun captain lit the fuse, the men jumped out of the way and covered their ears. The violent explosion blasted the cannon backward into the ship. The crew immediately leaped forward to reload.

TYPES OF SHOT

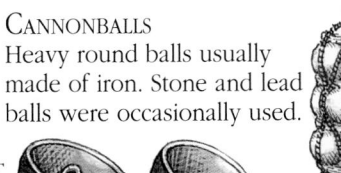

CANNONBALLS
Heavy round balls usually made of iron. Stone and lead balls were occasionally used.

CHAIN SHOT
Heavy balls joined by a chain. They tangled in the enemy ship's rigging and tore it down.

GRAPE SHOT
Iron balls, each the size of a tennis ball, bound in canvas bags.

CANISTER SHOT
Cylindrical cases containing pistol balls. They were used at close range to kill people.

Breastwork
In battle, the crew rolled up the ship's hammocks and stuffed them into the nets on the upper decks. This formed a wall called "breastwork" to provide some protection from enemy musket fire. Cannon shot could go right through, however!

Firing chain shot
By elevating the guns, the crew aimed chain shot at the enemy ship's rigging.

Splinters
A direct hit on the gun deck created a shower of deadly flying splinters, scattering the terrified crew. Many would be killed instantly.

Double-shotting
To make holes in the enemy ship, crews loaded two balls in the cannon with plenty of powder. This was called "double-shotting."

Plugging holes
When the enemy scored a direct hit at the waterline, the carpenters got to work. They rushed along the carpenters' walk – a special corridor that provided easy access for repairs – with their tools, and quickly nailed timbers or sheets of lead over the hole. Surprisingly few ships were actually sunk by cannon fire.

Shot splash

Survivors clinging to wreckage

Job hazards
The crews loading, aiming, and firing the guns faced instant death or horrible injuries. They could be killed or have limbs severed by cannon shot, crushed by an out-of-control gun, or badly cut by flying splinters from a direct hit. Accounts of battle also tell of crew members being instantly cut in half or decapitated (heads cut off) by shot.

Shot garlands
Rusty cannon balls were scraped, greased, and stored in special racks called shot garlands.

Keep your powder dry!
Powder monkeys rushed the dangerous cartridges of gunpowder from the handling chamber along the narrow gangways and ladders to the guns. They were helped in this dangerous task by just about anyone else not manning a gun – including any women on board.

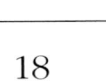

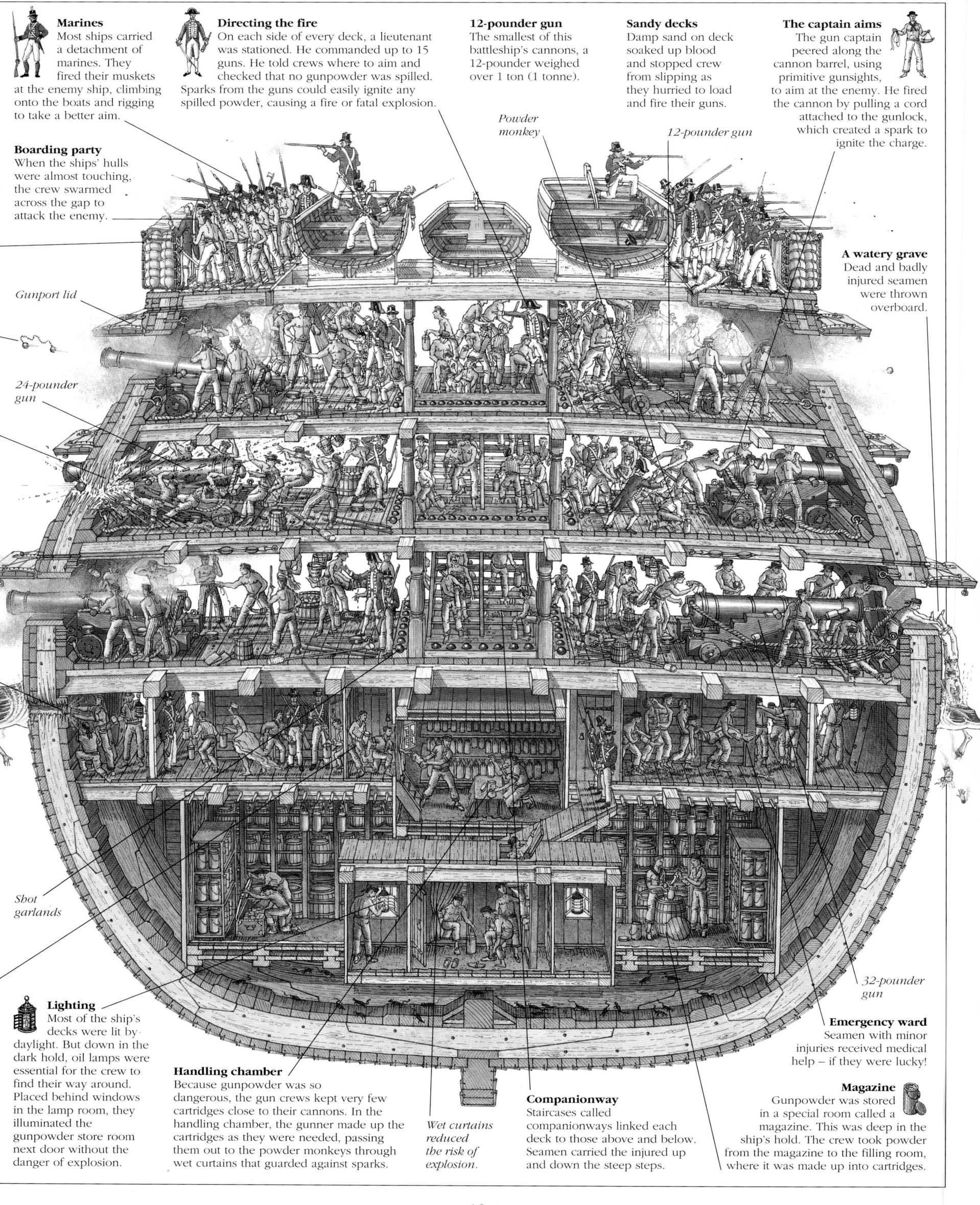

Marines
Most ships carried a detachment of marines. They fired their muskets at the enemy ship, climbing onto the boats and rigging to take a better aim.

Directing the fire
On each side of every deck, a lieutenant was stationed. He commanded up to 15 guns. He told crews where to aim and checked that no gunpowder was spilled. Sparks from the guns could easily ignite any spilled powder, causing a fire or fatal explosion.

12-pounder gun
The smallest of this battleship's cannons, a 12-pounder weighed over 1 ton (1 tonne).

Sandy decks
Damp sand on deck soaked up blood and stopped crew from slipping as they hurried to load and fire their guns.

The captain aims
The gun captain peered along the cannon barrel, using primitive gunsights, to aim at the enemy. He fired the cannon by pulling a cord attached to the gunlock, which created a spark to ignite the charge.

Boarding party
When the ships' hulls were almost touching, the crew swarmed across the gap to attack the enemy.

Powder monkey

12-pounder gun

A watery grave
Dead and badly injured seamen were thrown overboard.

Gunport lid

24-pounder gun

Shot garlands

32-pounder gun

Lighting
Most of the ship's decks were lit by daylight. But down in the dark hold, oil lamps were essential for the crew to find their way around. Placed behind windows in the lamp room, they illuminated the gunpowder store room next door without the danger of explosion.

Handling chamber
Because gunpowder was so dangerous, the gun crews kept very few cartridges close to their cannons. In the handling chamber, the gunner made up the cartridges as they were needed, passing them out to the powder monkeys through wet curtains that guarded against sparks.

Wet curtains reduced the risk of explosion.

Companionway
Staircases called companionways linked each deck to those above and below. Seamen carried the injured up and down the steep steps.

Emergency ward
Seamen with minor injuries received medical help – if they were lucky!

Magazine
Gunpowder was stored in a special room called a magazine. This was deep in the ship's hold. The crew took powder from the magazine to the filling room, where it was made up into cartridges.

SLEEPING

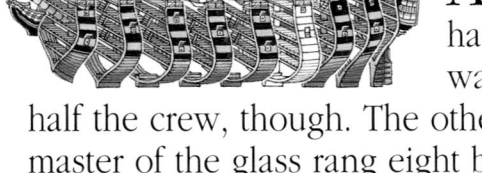

AT NIGHT, shipboard life slowed down. Sailors had to be in their hammocks by the start of first watch (8 o'clock). This was bedtime for only half the crew, though. The other half stood watch until midnight, when the master of the glass rang eight bells. The bells signaled the start of the second watch, and the two teams changed over. This system meant that most sailors got no more than four hours sleep at a time. However, it had advantages. Navy rules limited hammocks to 14 in (37 cm) in width. But with half the crew on watch, those in their hammocks had double the sleeping space. Things got very crowded, however, in port. There, only a few sailors stood watch, and the mass of sleeping bodies made the lower decks very stuffy. In the morning, the air was so foul that waking sailors felt like they had slept with mouths full of copper coins. They called this feeling "fat head."

THE ART OF THE HAMMOCK

Unroll hammock and hang it between two beams.

Add blankets and swing right leg up, balancing with left hand.

With a jump and a twist, spring into hammock – but don't fall out the other side!

Getting into a hammock looked difficult, but it was an art that every seaman learned quickly. Getting out was more difficult, especially if the occupant was asleep when the boatswain's mate came to wake him. "Out or down!" he'd cry. "Out or down" was a threat to cut down the hammocks of the last sailors to get up – a painful drop down onto the hard deck below!

ROLL THOSE HAMMOCKS!
When not in use, hammocks were rolled up. Sailors then had to pass their hammocks through an iron ring to make sure that they were rolled tightly enough.

DRUMMING DAYBREAK

Gun fires to signal sunrise

When the ship was at anchor with the rest of the fleet, there was a careful ritual to follow every morning. At first light, a drummer on board each ship began to beat his drum; this continued until it was light enough "to see a gray goose at a mile." Then the flagship fired a gun. When the sun rose, each ship hauled up its colors (flags).

THE NIGHT WATCH

A lighted box called a binnacle enclosed the ship's two compasses.

A special night telescope was used – but the image it showed was upside down!

Seeing clearly in the dark at sea was difficult. However, on the open sea when there were no other ships nearby, it was possible to sail safely at night without fear of collision or grounding on rocks. Lanterns lit the ship's two compasses so that the quartermaster could see in which direction the ship was headed. At night, the watch used a special telescope, called a "night glass," for a brighter image than with a "day glass."

Taking prisoners
Taking prisoners in battle was inconvenient: they had to be fed just like the crew – and guarded too. However, there was often a bounty (prize money) for prisoners. This could add up to quite a large sum, so capturing prisoners was worthwhile. During long wars, the two sides sometimes exchanged prisoners. This was another reason to keep enemy sailors alive.

A scrub in the tub
Prisoners were often in a filthy state when they were captured. They got a bath not just because they smelled, but because they were a health risk for the crew.

Short back and sides
Lice could easily introduce disease to the ship. The barber shaved the heads of the prisoners to reduce this risk.

New clothes
The purser's mate issued prisoners with clothes up to the value of the bounty they were worth.

Asleep on biscuits
Small hammock mattresses were called biscuits because they resembled ship's biscuits in shape and color.

Blanket Bay
Seamen had many nicknames for their hammocks and for sleeping. "Blanket Bay" is one nickname with obvious origins.

Sold before the mast
If a seaman died, his messmates "sold his possessions before the mast" – they auctioned off his belongings. The proceeds went to the man's family, so out of generosity everybody paid far more than the goods were really worth.

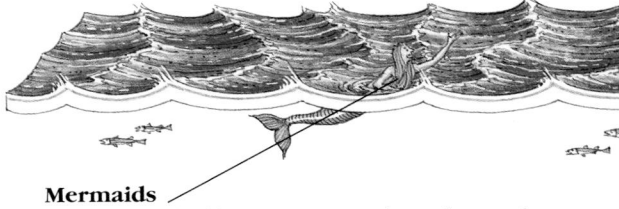

Mermaids
Sailors who had been at sea too long dreamed about seeing beautiful half-women, half-fish creatures called mermaids in the waves alongside the ship.

Midshipman's mess
Only the purser and surgeon were supposed to sleep on the orlop deck, but it was a popular place to sling a hammock. Though there was no natural light and little air, the orlop deck was spacious and quiet compared with the gun decks above.

Chain pump
Leather washers fixed to a ring-shaped chain formed an efficient pump. Pulling on the chain sucked water out of the bilges and sent it flowing down the "pump dale" – a gulley that crossed the gun deck. However, if a cannonball holed the ship below the waterline, the sea leaked in as quickly as it could be pumped out. Then the crew had to man the pumps day and night, until the carpenters could make a repair.

Smallest servants
The youngest "officer's servants" were no more than eight years old and so small that they had to be lifted into their hammocks to sleep.

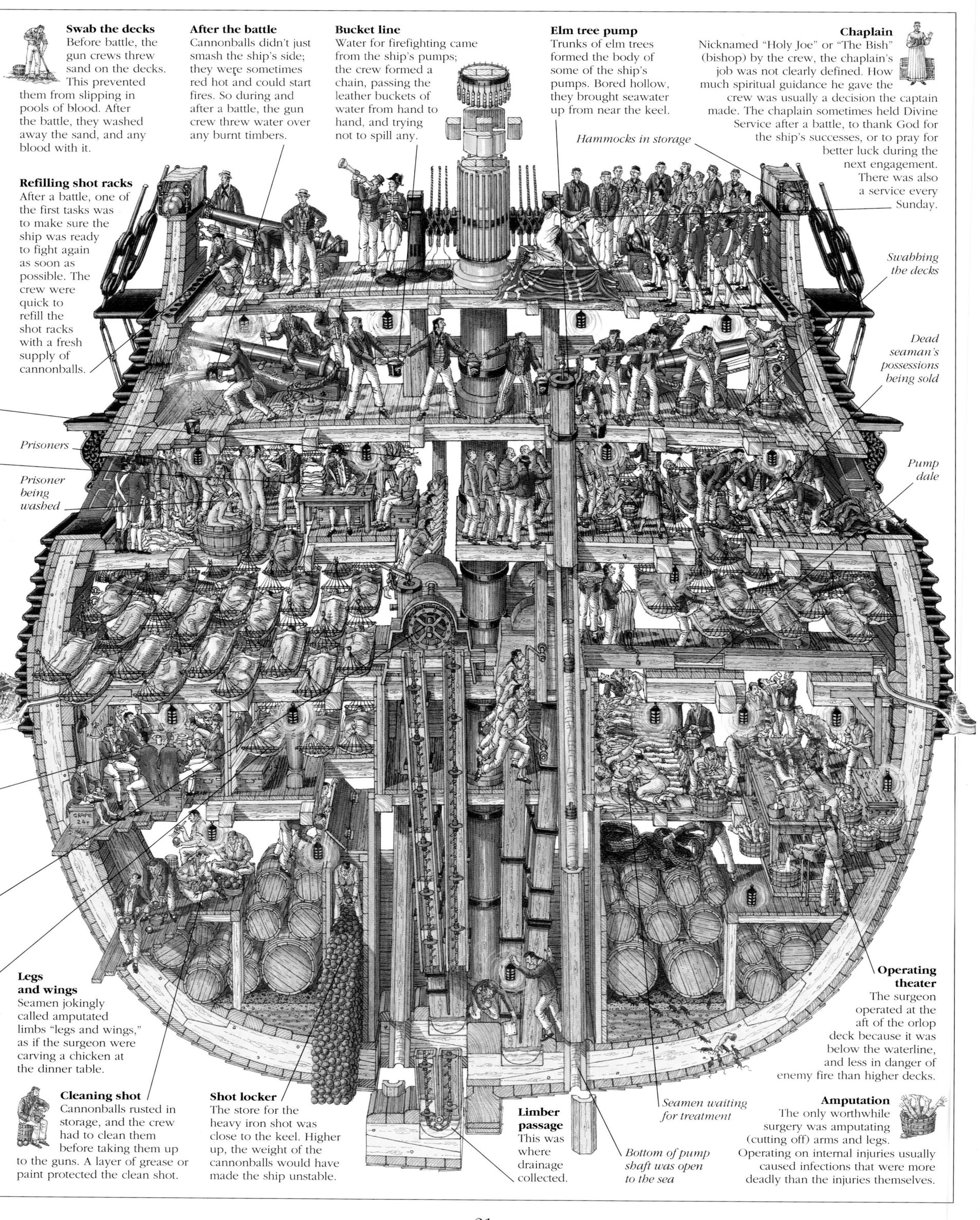

Swab the decks
Before battle, the gun crews threw sand on the decks. This prevented them from slipping in pools of blood. After the battle, they washed away the sand, and any blood with it.

After the battle
Cannonballs didn't just smash the ship's side; they were sometimes red hot and could start fires. So during and after a battle, the gun crew threw water over any burnt timbers.

Bucket line
Water for firefighting came from the ship's pumps; the crew formed a chain, passing the leather buckets of water from hand to hand, and trying not to spill any.

Elm tree pump
Trunks of elm trees formed the body of some of the ship's pumps. Bored hollow, they brought seawater up from near the keel.

Chaplain
Nicknamed "Holy Joe" or "The Bish" (bishop) by the crew, the chaplain's job was not clearly defined. How much spiritual guidance he gave the crew was usually a decision the captain made. The chaplain sometimes held Divine Service after a battle, to thank God for the ship's successes, or to pray for better luck during the next engagement. There was also a service every Sunday.

Hammocks in storage

Refilling shot racks
After a battle, one of the first tasks was to make sure the ship was ready to fight again as soon as possible. The crew were quick to refill the shot racks with a fresh supply of cannonballs.

Swabbing the decks

Dead seaman's possessions being sold

Prisoners

Prisoner being washed

Pump dale

Legs and wings
Seamen jokingly called amputated limbs "legs and wings," as if the surgeon were carving a chicken at the dinner table.

Cleaning shot
Cannonballs rusted in storage, and the crew had to clean them before taking them up to the guns. A layer of grease or paint protected the clean shot.

Shot locker
The store for the heavy iron shot was close to the keel. Higher up, the weight of the cannonballs would have made the ship unstable.

Limber passage
This was where drainage collected.

Bottom of pump shaft was open to the sea

Seamen waiting for treatment

Operating theater
The surgeon operated at the aft of the orlop deck because it was below the waterline, and less in danger of enemy fire than higher decks.

Amputation
The only worthwhile surgery was amputating (cutting off) arms and legs. Operating on internal injuries usually caused infections that were more deadly than the injuries themselves.

Navigation and Discipline

PUNISHING DISOBEDIENT SAILORS and guiding the ship's course were among the captain's most difficult duties – but for very different reasons. To keep the ship running smoothly, the captain had to punish those who did not obey orders, often by flogging (whipping). Navy rules gave captains a lot of latitude in choosing the amount of punishment for an offender. If a captain ordered too few lashes, the crew would think he was weak. A captain who ordered too many lashes was equally unpopular.

Navigation was tricky because charts (sea maps) were often inaccurate, and instruments primitive. Officers could accurately estimate how far the ship had traveled north or south, but reckoning how far the ship had sailed east or west was harder. An error of just a few miles at the end of a long ocean journey could wreck a ship on jagged rocks.

Offender in leg irons

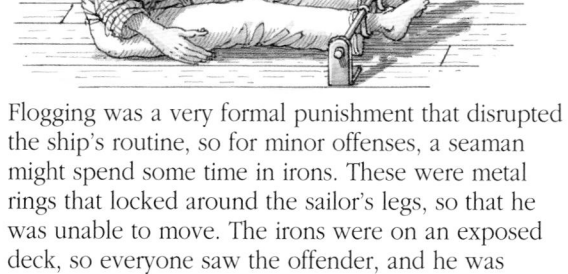

Flogging was a very formal punishment that disrupted the ship's routine, so for minor offenses, a seaman might spend some time in irons. These were metal rings that locked around the sailor's legs, so that he was unable to move. The irons were on an exposed deck, so everyone saw the offender, and he was scorched by the sun and soaked by rain and spray.

Shot rolling

Ships on the verge of mutiny were known in the navy as "shot-rolling ships." This was because discontented crew members tried to knock unwary officers off their feet by sending cannonballs rolling along the deck. Shot-rolling ships usually became that way because the captain ordered too many punishments.

Logbook

The ship's logbook was a sort of daily diary kept by the captain of the ship. In it he wrote the ship's position in degrees of latitude (distance north or south) and longitude (distance east or west). He also recorded the weather conditions and barometric pressure, as well as daily events such as floggings, what ports the ship visited, changes to the ship's course, and any actions the ship took part in.

Navigation equipment

All ships carried basic navigation equipment, including a compass, sextant, set of charts, and a log line. The first three helped the captain work out the ship's position and course, although charts were often wrong. The log line measured the speed at which the ship was sailing.

Ship's compass
The compass was the principal instrument for navigation. The printed card covered a magnetized needle that pointed north, helping the captain and crew find their way.

Log line
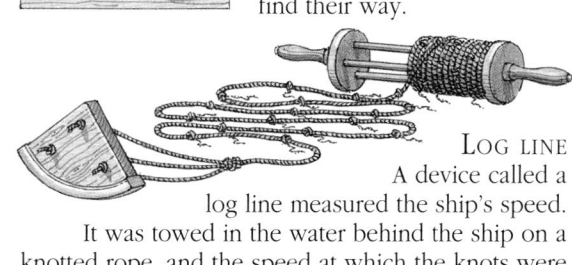
A device called a log line measured the ship's speed. It was towed in the water behind the ship on a knotted rope, and the speed at which the knots were paid out was noted. This is the origin of the nautical measurement of speed: "knots."

Sextant
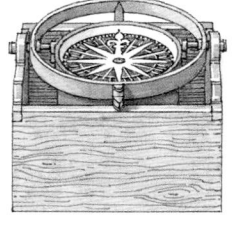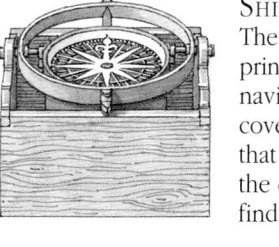
The sextant was a navigational instrument developed from an earlier, similar-looking device called an octant. Sextants measured the sun's height at noon. Using this measurement, sailors could calculate how far north or south the ship was.

Charts
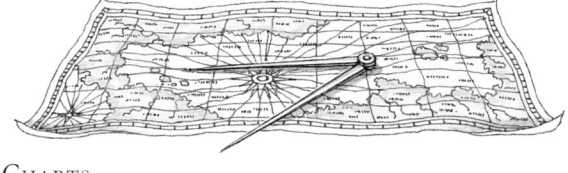
Charts showed islands, rocks and reefs, coastlines, and landmarks such as lighthouses. In 1800, many charts were still wildly inaccurate, showing, for example, islands where none existed.

Fire buckets
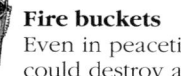
Even in peacetime, an accidental fire could destroy a ship, so fire buckets were always handy. Buckets of sand alternated with buckets of water.

Running the gauntlet
Thieves were unpopular, and the whole crew punished them. Everyone found a piece of rope and formed two lines. The thief walked between the lines as his shipmates whipped him. To stop the thief from going too fast, the master at arms walked in front with his cutlass (short sword) touching the man's belly. A marine walked behind with his bayonet on the man's back, to stop him from going too slowly. Running the gauntlet was abolished in 1806.

Gun drill
The crew trained regularly so that they could load and fire the guns rapidly. Officers timed them – the fastest gun crews took ninety seconds a shot.

Fighting
Fights often broke out when seamen had drunk too much rum. The boatswain's mates broke up the fights with their rattans (small cane whips).

Left hand down a bit
Steering the ship was the job of the quartermaster. The wheel turned a wooden drum, and ropes wrapped around the drum moved the tiller as the quartermaster turned the wheel.

Getting a checked shirt
Flogging made a diamond pattern of deep bloody cuts across the victim's back. The seamen's lighthearted nickname for the scars – "a checked shirt" – helped them forget the pain of the flogging.

Flogging around the fleet
The worst punishment of all was "flogging around the fleet." The offender was tied to capstan bars in the ship's largest boat and rowed around every ship of the fleet. Boatswain's mates from each ship whipped the man about 24 times, so that, in all, he received as many as 300 lashes. A doctor stood by to check that the flogging did not kill the man immediately. If he fainted, the rest of the punishment was delayed until he recovered. Most victims later died.

Spitting on deck
Smoking was a fire hazard, so seamen chewed tobacco instead, spitting it out into a small tub called a spitkid. Seamen who spat on deck were tied up with the spitkid round their necks. Then their messmates played target practice!

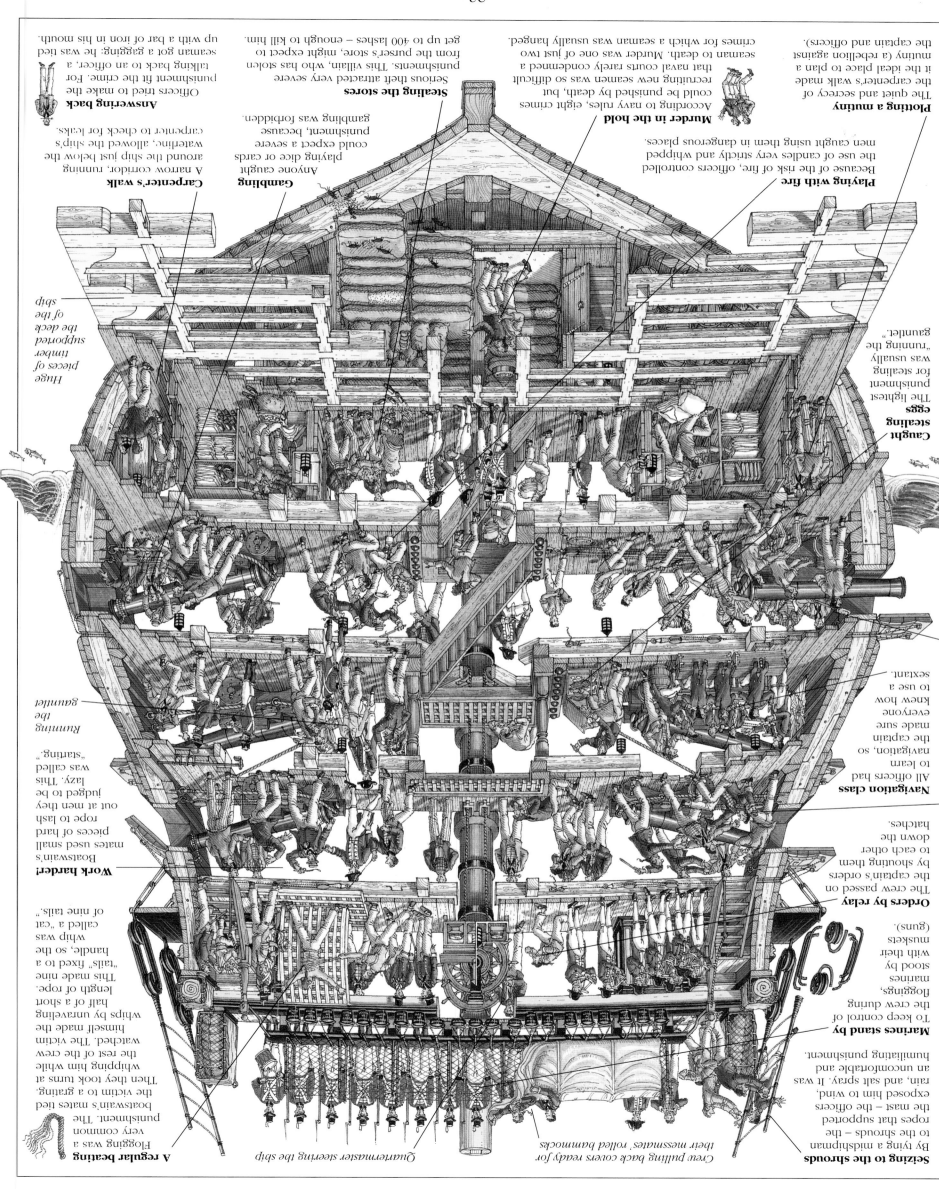

Plotting a mutiny
The quiet and secrecy of the carpenter's walk made it the ideal place to plan a mutiny (a rebellion against the captain and officers).

Murder in the hold
According to navy rules, eight crimes could be punished by death, but recruiting new seamen was so difficult that naval courts rarely condemned a seaman to death. Murder was one of just two crimes for which a seaman was usually hanged.

Stealing the stores
Serious theft attracted very severe punishments. This villain, who has stolen from the purser's store, might expect to get up to 400 lashes – enough to kill him.

Gambling
Anyone caught playing dice or cards could expect a severe punishment, because gambling was forbidden.

Carpenter's walk
A narrow corridor, running around the ship just below the waterline, allowed the ship's carpenter to check for leaks.

Answering back
Officers tried to make the punishment fit the crime. For talking back to an officer, a seaman got a gagging; he was tied up with a bar of iron in his mouth.

Playing with fire
Because of the risk of fire, officers controlled the use of candles very strictly and whipped men caught using them in dangerous places.

Huge pieces of timber supported the deck of the ship

Caught stealing eggs
The lightest punishment for stealing was usually "running the gauntlet."

"running the gauntlet."

Navigation class
All officers had to learn navigation, so the captain made sure everyone knew how to use a sextant.

Orders by relay
The crew passed on the captain's orders by shouting them to each other down the hatches.

Marines stand by
To keep control of the crew during floggings, marines stood by with their muskets (guns).

Seizing to the shrouds
By tying a midshipman to the shrouds – the ropes that supported the mast – the officers exposed him to wind, rain, and salt spray. It was an uncomfortable and humiliating punishment.

Running the gauntlet

Work harder!
Boatswain's mates used small pieces of hard rope to lash out at men they judged to be lazy. This was called "starting."

A regular beating
Flogging was a very common punishment. The boatswain's mates tied the victim to a grating. Then they took turns at whipping him while the rest of the crew watched. The victim himself made the whips by unraveling half of a short length of rope. This made nine "tails" fixed to a handle, so the whip was called a "cat of nine tails."

Crew pulling back covers ready for their messmates' rolled hammocks

Quartermaster steering the ship

THE OFFICERS

A MAN-OF-WAR was like a small city floating in a wooden box. On board there were many kinds of people, ranging from wealthy gentlemen down to laborers. Ruling over the whole ship was the captain (or the admiral on a flagship). He was powerful, but he did not command the ship alone. He had officers to help him. The most important were the lieutenants. Below the lieutenants was a large range of warrant officers. The lowest, such as sailmaker, was hardly higher in rank than a rating (an ordinary sailor).

When the captain issued an order, such as "Follow that ship!," each officer interpreted that order. The first lieutenant might shout "steer to port" to the quartermaster; the quartermaster then looked at the compass and shouted "Five points to port" to his mate who turned the wheel. This was called the ship's chain of command. Disobedient sailors were severely punished.

WHO WAS WHO ON BOARD

MARINES—There were 131 privates of marines (soldiers who fought at sea).

CAPTAIN LIEUTENANT SERGEANT'S CORPORALS DRUMMERS

SEAMEN There were 569 ratings, or ordinary seamen, on board. They were organized into two "watches."

IDLERS Steward's mate, Carpenter's crew, Sailmaker's crew made and mended the sails.

INFERIOR WARRANT OFFICERS Chaplain, Cook, Schoolmaster, 5 Surgeon's mates, Armorer repaired and maintained not only weapons, but all the ship's metalwork. Master-at-arms instructed the crew in the use of small arms (hand guns and muskets). Sailmaker repaired the sails.

PETTY OFFICERS Steward, Captain's Clerk, 4 Yeoman of the sheets kept the sails in order, Trumpeter, 6 Quartermasters' mates, 6 Quartermasters responsible for steering the ship and keeping lookout, 6 Master mates, 4 Boatswain's mates, 2 Gunner's mates, 2 Carpenter's mates, 24 Midshipmen trainee officers, 25 Quarter Gunners each in charge of four guns, Sailmaker's mate, 2 Corporals assistants to the master-at-arms, Coxwain looked after the ship's boats and steered them.

WARRANT SEA OFFICERS Master navigated the ship and piloted (guided) it close to the coast and on rivers. Boatswain storesman and administrator, responsible for the rigging and sails. Gunner in charge of all the cannons, Carpenter, Surgeon, Purser in charge of supplies.

LIEUTENANTS Assisted the captain in carrying out orders and directing gunfire in battle.

1st LIEUTENANT The captain's assistant, commanding the ship in his absence or if be was killed.

CAPTAIN Commanded the ship. Responsible for sailing, discipline, and battle command.

ADMIRAL Commanded the fleet and worked out battle plans.

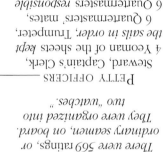

Gunroom
The stern end of the lower deck was called the gun room. It was used as a store for hand weapons such as cutlasses and pistols.

Paneled partitions
The captain's accommodation was paneled like a fine country house of the time. However, the guns in the "dining room" were a reminder that this was a fighting ship. Before a battle, the crew removed all the paneling. They either stowed it in the hold or, in an emergency, threw the panels overboard. This turned the captain's suite of rooms into an extension of the gun deck.

Officer's cabin
Commissioned (senior) officers had a little space of their own between the guns on the middle deck. How much room they had varied greatly from ship to ship.

Washstand
The captain's handy washstand had a chamber pot in a drawer hidden in the base for his convenience at night. A servant emptied it over the side in the morning.

Admiral's dining cabin
The admiral entertained in style. He had a grander dining room than even the captain. The paneling and furniture were folded neatly away in the preparation for battle.

Boat fall

The ship's boats were used to ferry the captain and other officers to shore.

Dinner for one
The captain's life was a lonely one. A captain was expected to be firm with his men, not friendly. Captains who tried to be popular quickly lost the respect of their crew. The captain dined alone, unless he was eating with the ship's officers in the wardroom or entertaining them in his own dining room. However, only a wealthy captain could afford to do this often.

"Heave to"
There were only two ways to communicate with other ships and boats: by shouting ("heave to" meant "stop immediately") or by using flags (see next page).

Hanging cot
The captain slept in a boxlike cot that hung from the deckhead (ceiling). It's no coincidence that the cot looks like a coffin: it was made to fit the sleeper, and if he died, he was nailed into it with some shot. The crew heaved the cot-coffin over the side, complete with cannonballs and captain, and it sank like a stone.

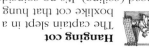

You rang, Sir?
Commissioned officers took servants to sea with them. Every officer could have one servant, and some were entitled to two. The captain was allowed four servants for each 100 members of the ship's crew. Though they were called servants, they were actually more like apprentices – young gentlemen studying the craft of their master.

Bread room
This part of the orlop deck was a store for the ship's biscuits. The navy called them navy bread, so the store was the bread room.

Rude awakening
The schoolmaster was lucky if he could hang his hammock in the tiny space at the side of the tiller sweep. However, young midshipmen made sure that he wasn't comfortable for long!

Schoolroom
The chaplain used the gun-room to teach the youngest midshipmen (trainee officers) about the Bible.

Officer's cabin servants at work

Maintaining the davits
Exposed to the salt spray on an open deck, the davits needed constant attention. If one of the tackles jammed while the boat was being lowered, it would dump the boat crew into the water.

Poop deck

Skylight
This provided natural light for the captain's dining cabin.

Schoolroom

Oak paneling

Foothold cleats
Blocks of wood called cleats provided footholds for climbing into the boats.

Lowering the boats
The ship's sides bulged out close to the waterline, so davits (cranes) were needed to lower the boats to the water.

Captain's sleeping cabin
The captain had the luxury of space and privacy. He had a separate bedroom, screened off from his dining room by bulkheads.

Wash-stand

Admiral's dining cabin

Boat fall
The tackle used to lower the boat was called the boat fall. The arrangement of pulleys made the job of hauling the boat out of the water easier.

Officer's cabin

Gun room

Bath time!
Washing was a rare treat on a man-of-war, even the admiral could have the luxury of a bath only once a week or so. His servants heated rainwater on a portable stove (soap didn't work with seawater).

Canvas wall
The canvas screen separating the cabin from the wardroom next door provided little privacy.

Gooseneck
When the quartermaster turned the ship's wheel, the gooseneck, which supported the tiller, swung across the gunroom. To allow for this movement, much of the gunroom was empty. The empty area was called the tiller sweep.

Down the hatch
None of the officers drank water with dinner, because after a month or two at sea it tasted terrible. Officers drank as much alcohol (and often more than) the seamen. When one man-of-war captured a foreign ship laden with wine, some of the officers were drinking half a gallon of wine (2 quarts, or 2.27 liters) every day.

All dressed up
The admiral's uniform was very grand. Other officers were allowed to wear dress uniforms, but they didn't always want to. The uniform was expensive (an officer had to pay for it out of his own pay) and hard to keep clean.

Good spirits
The heaviest provisions were always stowed as low as possible. The spirit room contained wines and spirits.

Poop deck
The highest deck at the stern (back) of the ship was called the poop deck. It got its name from the ships of ancient Rome: their stern deck was called a *puppis*.

Wardroom
Commissioned officers ate in the wardroom. They also relaxed here and played games or musical instruments. The wardroom was a lively place.

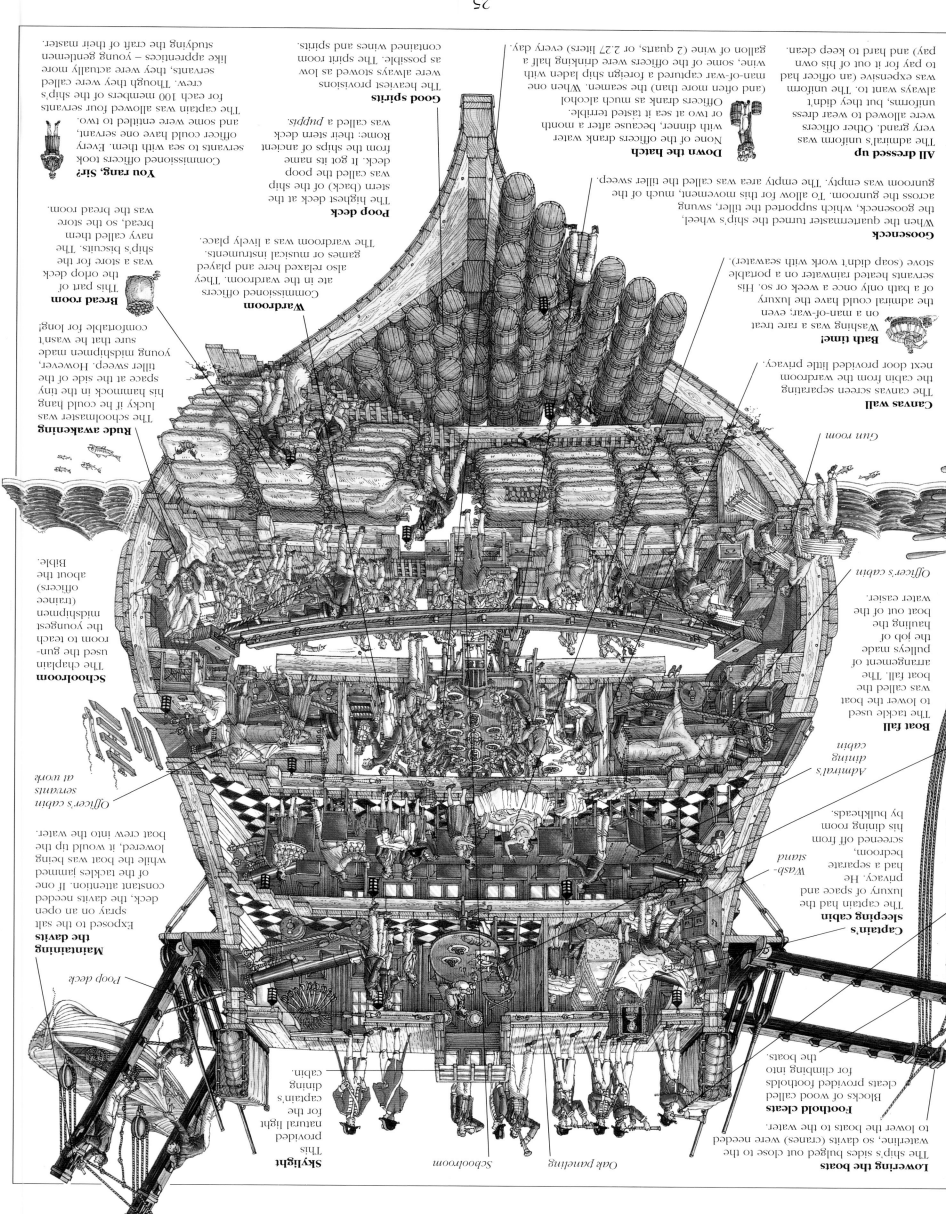

THE ADMIRAL

A MAN-OF-WAR rarely sailed on its own. Usually, it cruised with a group of similar and smaller ships. Together they sailed as a fleet, with an admiral in command. Admirals were chosen from among the best captains. The post of admiral was the highest in the navy, and it was a very responsible job. When there was a victory, the admiral took much of the credit. In defeat, he took the blame. If the admiral made the wrong decision, he would be in trouble when the fleet returned to port. But while at sea, there was no quick way to get messages back to the Admiralty (the government department in charge of the navy). In return for all this responsibility, the admiral was richly rewarded. He lived well in the ship, with his own cook and as many as 20 servants. When the fleet captured an enemy ship, the admiral got a one-eighth share of the prize.

THE NAVAL SALUTE

Tar-covered palm

Every sailor greeted a senior officer with a salute, but the admiral got a particularly enthusiastic salute. The naval salute was unusual: the sailor held his palm turned in toward his face. This concealed his palm, which was blackened by tar from the ropes.

PRIZE MONEY

The admiral got a big share of all the prize money from the entire fleet.

Ordinary seamen (ratings) only got a small fraction of their ship's prize money.

After a victorious battle, the government awarded prizes equal to the value of the enemy ships captured. One-quarter of the prize was divided between all the seamen on the ship that made the capture. On a 100-gun ship, each rating thus got less than one two-thousandth of the prize. The admiral won one-eighth and the captain one-quarter. However, the captain received prize money only for vessels his ship captured, while the admiral got one-eighth of the prizes from *every* capture in the fleet. Admirals could get very rich this way.

FLAG SIGNALS

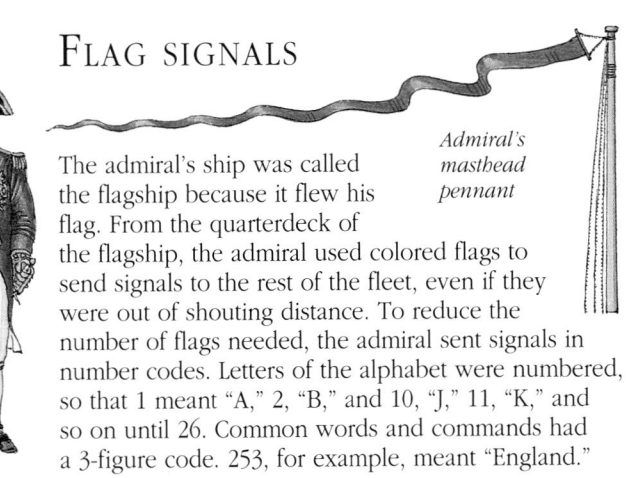

Admiral's masthead pennant

The admiral's ship was called the flagship because it flew his flag. From the quarterdeck of the flagship, the admiral used colored flags to send signals to the rest of the fleet, even if they were out of shouting distance. To reduce the number of flags needed, the admiral sent signals in number codes. Letters of the alphabet were numbered, so that 1 meant "A," 2, "B," and 10, "J," 11, "K," and so on until 26. Common words and commands had a 3-figure code. 253, for example, meant "England."

NELSON'S SIGNAL

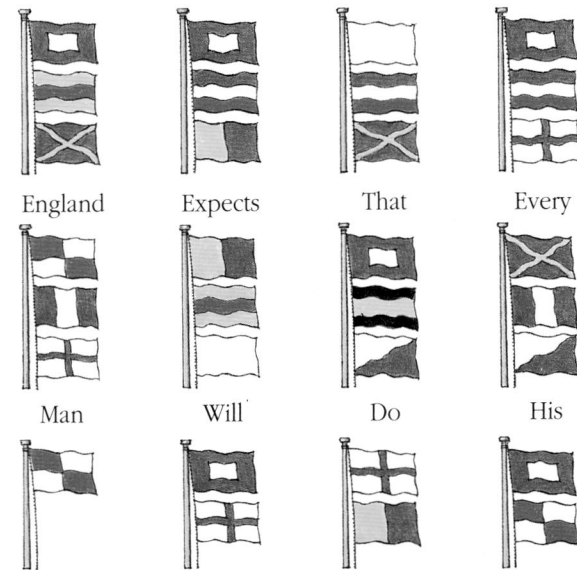

England	Expects	That	Every
Man	Will	Do	His
D	U	T	Y

Just before the Battle of Trafalgar in 1805, England's famous admiral, Horatio Nelson, sent a flag signal to cheer up his fleet. Nelson wanted to signal "England confides that every man will do his duty." However, his signal lieutenant, Mr. Pasco, suggested that "confides" was a difficult word. There was no number code for the word, so it would have had to be spelled out letter by letter. He suggested substituting "expects" – code 269 – so Nelson's signal appeared as above.

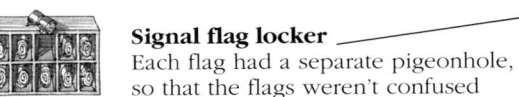

Signal flag locker
Each flag had a separate pigeonhole, so that the flags weren't confused when they were hoisted rapidly. Flags were stored carefully rolled in their compartments.

Cleaning duty
There was no water to flush the officers' lavatory in the quarter gallery, so cleaning it was not a popular job among the servants.

Fair or foul
The captain had to go on deck in all kinds of weather, so he kept an oilskin cape and boots handy.

Captain's day cabin
Like the captain's berth, his day cabin was at the stern of the ship. It was close to the wheel, so he could rush to take command in an emergency.

"Pieces of eight"
Some admirals owned caged parrots as souvenirs of trips across distant seas. The young midshipmen often taught the parrot to swear, call the admiral names, and say other rude things.

Admiral's barge
This was a long, light, narrow boat rowed by 10 or more oars. It was usually reserved for the personal use of the admiral.

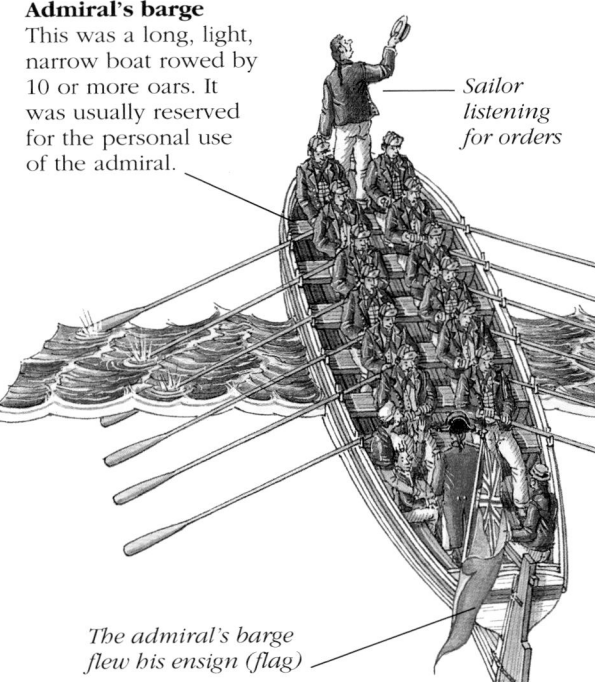

Sailor listening for orders

The admiral's barge flew his ensign (flag)

Quarter gallery
One of the quarter galleries at the far stern of the ship was the captain's lavatory. There were separate lavatories in the quarter galleries on lower decks for the other officers' use. The quarter galleries were decorated with colorful paint and carvings.

Admiral's day cabin
The admiral had an even more spacious day cabin than the captain. The "tiled" floor was actually a covering of stretched canvas painted with squares.

Furnishings
Captains could furnish their cabins as they pleased. Some lived in considerable luxury, fitting out their floating home just like a house on land. One captain turned his cabin into a library, so that it looked "more like a bookseller's shop than the captain's apartment in a man-of-war."

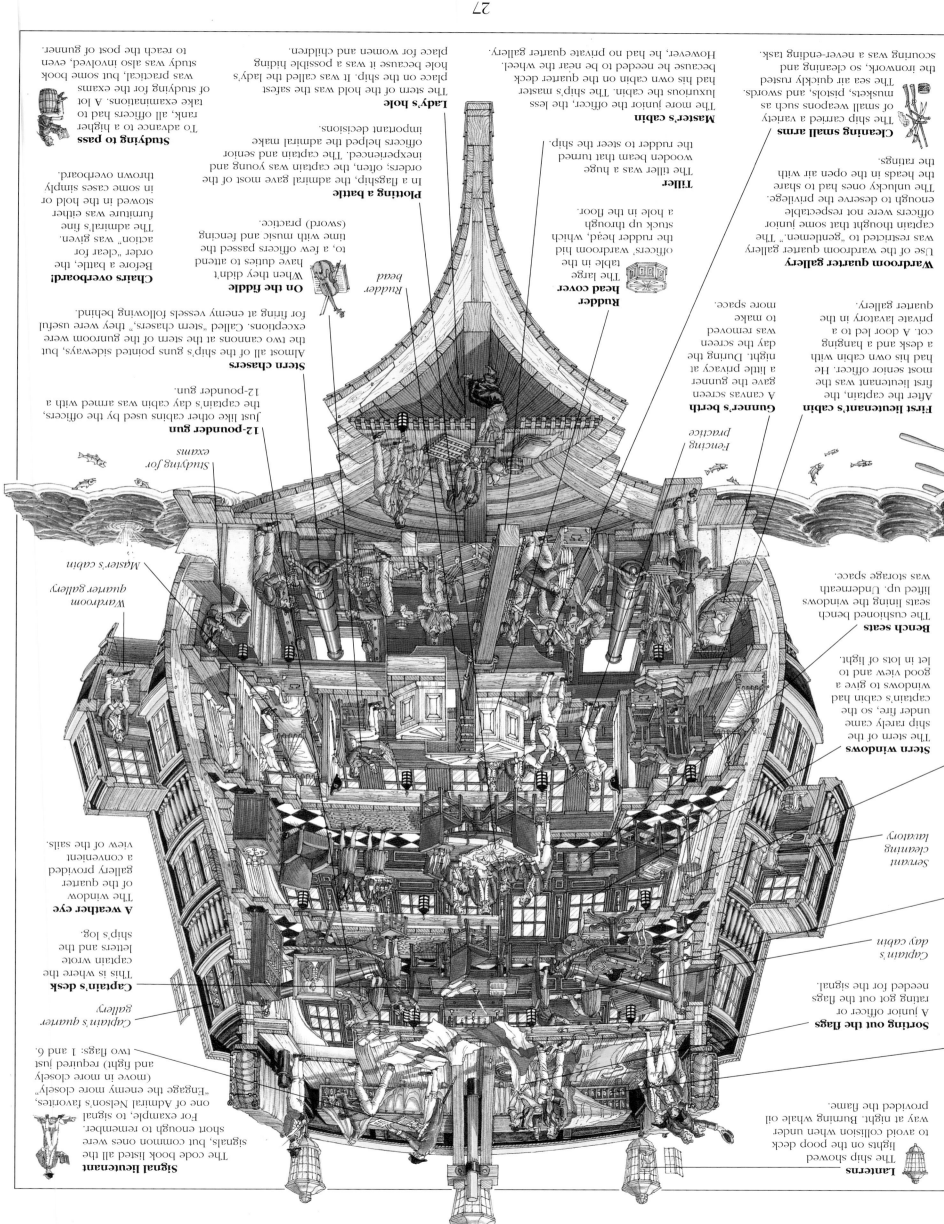

Cleaning small arms
The ship carried a variety of small weapons such as muskets, pistols, and swords. The sea quickly rusted the ironwork, so cleaning and scouring was a never-ending task.

Master's cabin
The more junior the officer, the less luxurious the cabin. The ship's master had his own cabin on the quarter deck because he needed to be near the wheel. However, he had no private quarter gallery.

Lady's hole
The stem of the hold was the safest place on the ship. It was called the lady's hole because it was a possible hiding place for women and children.

Studying to pass
To advance to a higher rank, all officers had to take examinations. A lot of studying for the exams was practical, but some book study was also involved, even to reach the post of gunner.

Plotting a battle
In a flagship, the admiral gave most of the orders; often, the captain was young and inexperienced. The captain and senior officers helped the admiral make important decisions.

On the fiddle
When they didn't have duties to attend to, a few officers passed the time with music and fencing (sword) practice.

Chairs overboard!
Before a battle, the order "clear for action" was given. The admiral's fine furniture was either stowed in the hold or in some cases simply thrown overboard.

Stern chasers
Almost all of the ship's guns pointed sideways, but the two cannons at the stern of the gunroom were exceptions. Called "stern chasers," they were useful for firing at enemy vessels following behind.

12-pounder gun
Just like other cabins used by the officers, the captain's day cabin was armed with a 12-pounder gun.

Studying for exams

Master's cabin

Wardroom quarter gallery

A weather eye
The window of the quarter gallery provided a convenient view of the sails.

Captain's desk
This is where the captain wrote letters and the ship's log.

Captain's quarter gallery

Signal lieutenant
The code book listed all the signals, but common ones were short enough to remember. For example, to signal one of Admiral Nelson's favorites, "Engage the enemy more closely" (move in more closely and fight) required just two flags: 1 and 6.

Wardroom quarter gallery
Use of the wardroom quarter gallery was restricted to "gentlemen." The captain thought that some junior officers were not respectable enough to deserve the privilege. The unlucky ones had to share the heads in the open air with the ratings.

First lieutenant's cabin
After the captain, the first lieutenant was the most senior officer. He had his own cabin with a desk and a hanging cot. A door led to a private lavatory in the quarter gallery.

Gunner's berth
A canvas screen gave the gunner a little privacy at night. During the day the screen was removed to make more space.

Bench seats
The cushioned bench seats lining the windows lifted up. Underneath was storage space.

Stern windows
The stern of the ship rarely came under fire, so the captain's cabin had windows to give a good view and to let in lots of light.

Servant cleaning lavatory

Captain's day cabin

Sorting out the flags
A junior officer or rating got out the flags needed for the signal.

Lanterns
The ship showed lights on the poop deck to avoid collision when under way at night. Burning whale oil provided the flame.

Tiller
The tiller was a huge wooden beam that turned the rudder to steer the ship.

Rudder head cover
The large table in the officers' wardroom hid the rudder head, which stuck up through a hole in the floor.

Rudder head

Fencing practice

Glossary

aft
Toward the rear of the ship.

aloft
High up above the deck in the rigging.

anchor
The heavy iron hook lowered to the seabed on a cable to stop the ship from drifting in shallow water.

ballast
Heavy weights at the bottom of the ship to keep it upright in the water.

bilges
The lowest part of a ship's hull; the bilges were filled with foul-smelling seawater.

bows
The front of the ship.

bulkhead
Wall inside the ship, usually below the waterline.

bunt
The middle of a sail, close to the mast.

capstan
Large drum-shaped winch that the crew turned to lift weights such as the anchor.

carronade
A type of short gun firing a heavy shot, first made by the Carron Ironworks of Scotland in the 1780s.

caulking
Plugging cracks between planks to make them waterproof.

charts
Sea maps.

compass
Magnetized needle that always pointed north, helping the crew find their way.

davit
On-board crane used mainly to lower boats.

flogging
Whipping as punishment.

fore
Toward the front of the ship.

galley
Ship's kitchen.

heads
Ship's lavatories used by seamen.

hold
Storage space low down in the ship.

hull
Main body of a ship.

keel
Long timber running along the whole length of the ship's base. It was the backbone of the ship.

larboard (or port)
The left side of the ship, looking forward.

leeward
The downwind side of the ship.

log
Ship captain's diary.

lubbers
Inexperienced sailors.

magazine
Special secure room near the bottom of ship where gunpowder was kept.

mast
One of the thick vertical poles to which the sails were attached.

mess
Group of seamen who shared their meals.

quarter galleries
Decorative projecting windows at the stern, which contained the officers' lavatories.

rigging
Ropes used to support and control the masts, yards, and sails.

rudder
Hinged flat structure attached to stern of the ship, which was turned to alter the ship's course (direction).

scurvy
Deadly disease caused by lack of fresh vegetables.

shot
Any kind of ammunition for cannon.

spanker
A small fore-and-aft rigged sail attached to the mizzen mast.

starboard
The right side of the ship, looking forward.

stern
The back of the ship.

tiller
Bar used to turn the rudder and thus guide the ship.

topmen
The crew members who worked on the highest sails.

watch
A period of duty, usually four hours long – or the members of the crew that worked it.

windward
The side of the ship that faced the wind.

yard
Horizontal beam fixed to the mast to support the sail.

yardarm
End of the yard.

Index

Acknowledgments
Dorling Kindersley would like to thank the following people:
The Commanding Officer of HMS *Victory* for assistance with research and background information
Sheila Hanly for editorial assistance
Lynn Bresler for the index

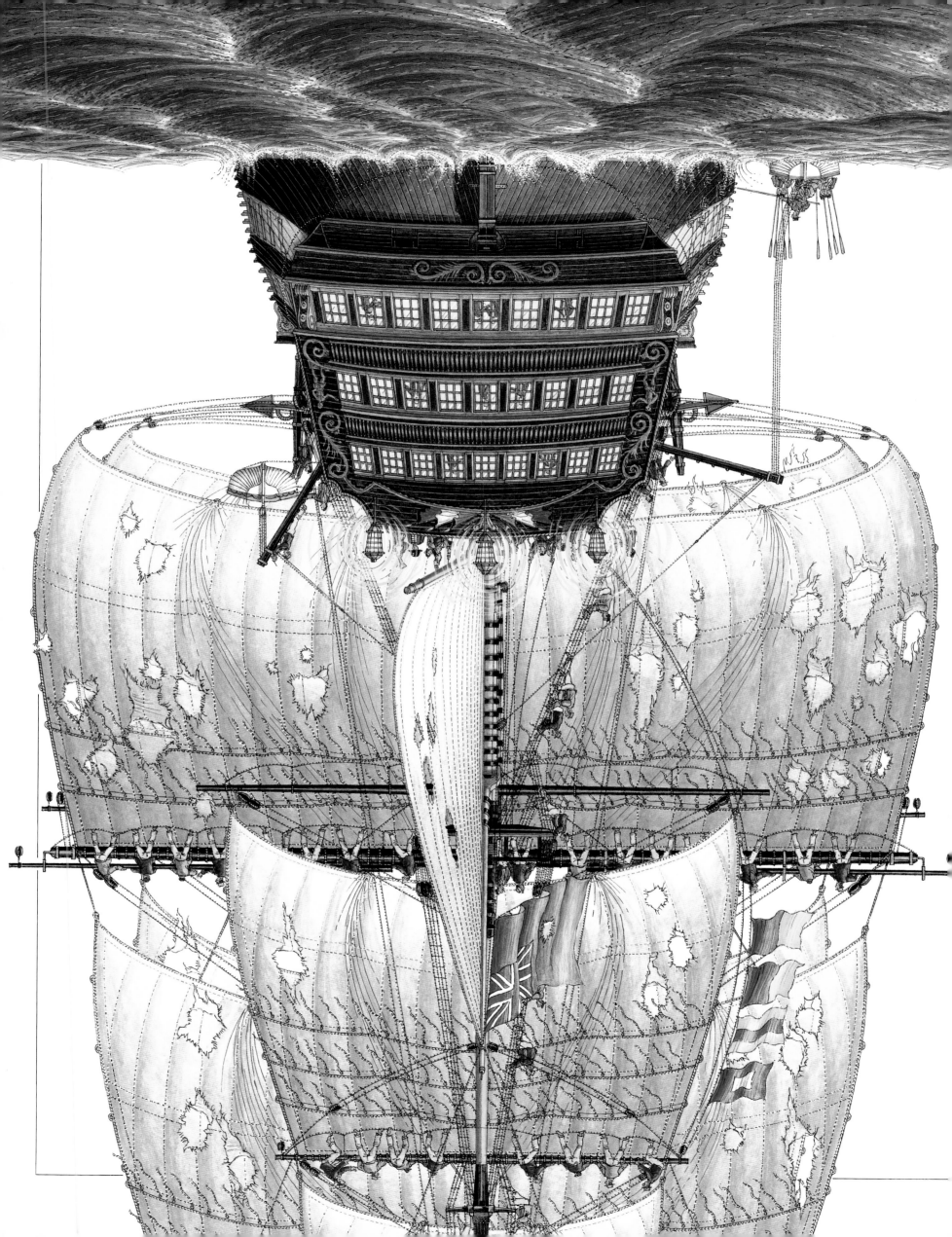

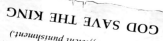

CAPTURED!

By the vigilance and fortitude of one

JACK NASTYFACE

a common rating

the STOWAWAY

was apprehended and brought before

THE CAPTAIN

The URCHIN was in a sorry state, having evaded the clutches of His Majesty's MARINES for a full week. The Captain took pity on the waif, and ordered the COOK to feed him up and the PURSER to clothe him.

The STOWAWAY is henceforth to serve

HIS MAJESTY

as a POWDER MONKEY *for a Twelvemonth until he can be deposited back at the port from whence he came. (This, and the ordeal he hath endured being considered sufficient punishment.)*

GOD SAVE THE KING